HOW A
"Truth Student"
Came to Know the Truth

MY RESCUE
FROM THE DECEPTION
OF THE NEW AGE

Taylor Bassett

ISBN 978-1-0980-9999-2 (paperback)
ISBN 978-1-63844-000-0 (digital)

Christian Faith Publishing, Inc.
832 Park Avenue
Meadville, PA 16335
www.christianfaithpublishing.com

Printed in the United States of America

Cover art by Pierre Ekladios

Contents

Preface

Dear reader, how would you feel if you learned that everything you'd ever been told about your life was a lie?

This book is about my life's journey that began under the falsehood of the New Age (which I sincerely believed and followed) to being awakened to the *real* truth that literally saved my soul. If you're the impatient type, you might want to skip ahead to the chapter "How My Achilles' Heel Was Exposed" and see how it happened for me. Otherwise, I invite you to see how God Almighty personally delivered, rescued, and transferred me from the false and damnable belief system of the New Age to the freeing and saving Gospel of eternal life and salvation through Jesus Christ.

As of this writing, I am sixty one years of age. For the first thirty-one years of my life, I was deceived into believing (and fervently practicing) the teachings of the New Age (specifically, the branch I'm referring to is called the Unity School of Christianity). What a disaster, but how was I to know? I always thought of myself as a Christian, and Unity always quoted the Holy Bible. It never occurred to me that they (as do all other false religions) were misquoting and misapplying the scriptures. Why would it occur to me? I had been raised in Unity, and it was all I ever knew.

It is not *only* Unity that teaches these precepts. Whether Unity (cofounded in 1889 by Charles and Myrtle Fillmore), Religious Science of the Mind (founded in 1927 by Ernest Holmes), Christian Science (founded in 1879 by Mary Baker Eddy), or any of the vast host of these offshoots, the basic teaching is the same.

> Control your thoughts. Control your life. You have a "mighty power within" that is just wait-

ing to deliver to your doorstep a life of health, wealth, and happiness; and it's all for the asking. They call this mighty power "the Christ of you." It is your "higher self" and is an individualization of the infinite divine mind that governs the universe.

In the New Age, God is *not* a personal being but rather a "creative principle."

Also, none of the New Agers listed above were original in their beliefs. They were all students of Phineas P. Quimby (February 16, 1802–January 16, 1866) who is known as the father of Christian Science, New Thought, and Unity. He was a hypnotist and believed in the "power of healing through suggestion."

Ironically, they consider themselves Christian organizations who love to quote and emphasize the Bible. I was so steeped in their writings that I thought I knew my Bible very well. But here's the most important question you'll ever answer: Of the sum total of your Christian knowledge, what percentage of it is owing to what somebody *told you* the Bible said versus what you've *actually read, in context,* for yourself? Your answer to that question will determine how susceptible you are to being deceived by cults and false religions, leading to a false worldview and eventually damnation.

The consequences are devastating and eternal. I know. I was in a cult which, if not for the grace of God, would have destroyed me. Oh, the myriad Bible verses I clung to! But I was clinging to what Unity *told* me they meant, *not* what they *actually* meant. Believe me, there's a difference! The difference is literally a matter of life and death, and it's *eternal* life and *eternal* death at that!

Do you know what's off-putting about labels and religion? It boxes you in. I realize there are many who prefer the word *spiritual* because that word has a very broad application and a more exciting feel. It doesn't lock them into organized religion. By their own admission, Unity prefers to "pull in truth from wherever they can find it"; thus, they take a little bit from all religions. But here's the rub. According to the Bible, there is only *one* salvation, one way to heaven, one life, and one truth. Now if there really *is* only one way, life, and truth, then all others would have to be false. There is no more serious issue than this because what's at stake is your soul.

I was 100 percent positive that I was on the right track. I would argue vehemently for my beliefs, and why not? The promises of the New Age were extremely enticing for someone who didn't know any better.

After all, what could be better than believing that your thoughts literally controlled your life and everything in it and that nobody but yourself is in control of those thoughts? That through the power of positive thinking, you actually create and attract all the health, wealth, and happiness you'd ever want? That your present lifetime is just one of many (perhaps thousands or millions) of lifetimes you live out in order to achieve your highest possible good? That the universe would bring to you all that was necessary to bring you ever closer to that great dawning of cosmic consciousness wherein you'd never again have to reincarnate and would be fully and completely happy? That through your higher self, you were attracting into your life persons, places, circumstances, and things that were solely designed to teach you your "highest good" before being whisked off to the next life? That you were fortunate to have matured to be able to grasp the "secret truths most of the world isn't ready to receive" and that your insight was the one and only correct one?

Growing up, I was always positive. I was brimming with positivity because I believed I really could accomplish anything through the power of thought! My imagination ran wild. And why did I really believe this? Because I was taught from as far back as I can remember the principles of the New Age that (according to them) rely on the ancient wisdom, the teachings of the Bible, and other "ascended masters." My positivity and sense of humor made me very likable among my friends. Being positive breeds confidence, and confidence has a quality all its own. People want to be around people who are positive and confident. It's a great vibe! Now there's nothing wrong with either being positive or having confidence unless you're positive and confident in a *falsehood!* That's doesn't help anybody! You can be 100 percent confident and positive that the laws of gravity don't apply to you right until the moment after you step off the roof. We all know how that's going to end. That person gets humbled immediately. They sincerely believed, but they sincerely believed *a lie*, and *all the sincerity in the world won't alter the truth*. The New Age would have them think that had they been "in tune," the accident would have never happened. This is because the New Age prescribes a doctrine known as *cause and effect*, which they believe follows universal laws.

This is what became of me in the New Age. It's very humbling to come to the point where you realize and accept that all you've learned, fervently believed to be true, and staked your very existence on is, in fact, a *lie*. The problem is that this false system is also mixed with a bit of truth, and it is that bit of truth that keeps the lie alive.

I wrote this book with two objectives in mind. First is that it might fall into the hands of someone struggling in the New Age and help them see what's really going on. Somebody once said, "There's nothing worse than climbing a ladder to get to the top of a building, only to discover the ladder is leaning against the *wrong* building!" The *truth* really will set you free, but first, you have to *know* the truth. And to be clear, *according to the Bible*, there is only one truth. "Oh, that's fine for me because I don't use the Bible," someone says. Then sadly, you'll never know the truth. You'll *think* you know the truth, but that just means you *think* you know the truth. That is not meant to be condescending. I felt the same way.

Second, I want to help anyone outside the New Age to better understand and empathize with the mindset and perspective of those who are *in* the New Age. I want to provide a useful tool in reaching them. After all, they're some of the nicest people you'll ever meet! But it's vitally important to understand that any biblical terms you use are read, received, and processed by the New Ager in a *completely different way* because the New Age assigns *different definitions* to them. This is where their deception begins. When a person believes such things as "there are many truths and paths leading to the same place of enlightenment" or when a person believes it is *perfectly acceptable* to *change* the meaning of the words from their original intent, it places them on a slippery slope that only leads to a false sense of well-being. This false sense of well-being leads to *eternal destruction*.

That was me. My go-to line would always be "Well, there are many interpretations of the Bible. After all, the Bible was written by men over the years and retranslated hundreds, if not thousands, of times. The Bible can be viewed literally, metaphysically, or spiritually, depending on your own level of spiritual growth and maturity. Moreover, what about all the alternate teachings from the great mystics and seers through the ages? What about the present-day channeling of beings who speak to us from other realms? Surely, we can't discount these valuable teachings and their depth of learning!" That argument certainly sounds compelling.

I count myself blessed to have been rescued from these errors and delivered into the everlasting truth by Almighty God. As we will see (and as I learned), the Bible *does not in any way* teach the precepts the New Age (or any other false religions system) claims it does. And regardless of how sincere a person may be, if something is wrong, it is wrong.

I pray this book will be an encouragement for many who are trapped in the New Age and also those wishing to reach them.

Acknowledgments

Without the following people, this book would never have been written:

My friend Arthur Cummins, your faithfulness to engage me over and over again in the thousands of hours of conversations we had both before and after my conversion speaks volumes and is something I shall never forget.

My son-in-law Pierre Ekladios, thank you for suggesting and encouraging me to write this book in the first place. Your push means more than you know.

My wife, Laura, your love, support, and never-ending encouragement have given me my own heaven on earth. I am so blessed to have such a wonderful Proverbs 31 woman as my wife.

The Lord Jesus Christ "who loved me and gave himself for me" (Galatians 2:20b).

My Introduction to the New Age

Let's start from the beginning. I was born on January 18, 1960, in Houston, Texas. My mother was a professional musician, and my father was a mechanical engineer. We moved a lot. My earliest remembrance is living in Portland, Oregon. We then moved to California and lived in Santa Clara and then Santa Cruz. I'm the youngest of four, which includes two half-brothers and a half-sister. My short life seemed normal until everything changed on February 27, 1967. That's the day my father died. We were living in Santa Cruz, California, at the time of his death; and I'd turned seven just a few weeks before. And it was then at the age of seven, I was introduced firsthand to something called death, and it was my own father who died.

What did this mean to me? It all started to hit me. My father would never be coming home from that hospital where I last visited him. I'd never see him again nor hear his voice. All the times when I'd rise early in the morning and sit with him at the breakfast table before he headed out to work were over. I'd no longer sit on his lap as we laughed ourselves silly watching the Roadrunner and Coyote cartoons. That bedside talk we had was still fresh in my mind. (I was five or six and had been crying pretty badly. After all, I was about to go from kindergarten to first grade, and some of my siblings had me terrified. They assured me that the carefree days of kindergarten were over. There was now going to be something called homework and that from now on, schooling was going to be very difficult. So I cried, and my father came in and consoled me. I could still hear his conversation with me as he calmed me down and helped me to stop crying.) *All these years later, I've used his very words to comfort and assure my own children*!

It was the evening of February 27, 1967, and now we were all gathered in the home of a neighbor who lovingly looked after us while our mother was at my father's bedside in the hospital. Mom arrived at the neighbor's home and quietly announced, "Family conference." We were shown to a smaller room. Whenever I heard *family conference*, it meant a big announcement was coming. Were we going to move? Were we getting another pet? Suddenly it got very quiet as we focused on my mother. Then with a quaking voice, she said, "Daddy died half an hour ago." There were gasps, but I really didn't know what to think. I figured as long as my siblings held it together, everything would be all right. I looked over and saw their tears, and I knew it was bad.

Naturally, we were devastated. While my head was spinning, I heard one of my siblings ask, "Why would God do that?" Now I'd heard about God but never quite grasped that idea. Apparently, he lived in heaven. My mother's answer would be something that affected me profoundly. It was what she had learned and believed from the New Age. Our mother explained that my dad "graduated." That is to say he'd gone to the "next plane of existence" where he'd spend time reviewing the lessons he'd learned during *this* lifetime in preparation for his reincarnation into his *next* lifetime. I was told that prior to his next incarnation, he (like all of us) would choose his parents ahead of time as well as all the other circumstances, events, and people that would benefit and prepare him for those lessons. These lessons would further him for the life he'd live after *that* which, in turn, prepared him for his next life after *that* and so on. All of this at the age of seven, I accepted it completely, and why wouldn't I? Children are very trusting.

These explanations had a very deep and far-reaching effect upon me. It certainly took the sting out of my father's death. I was suddenly aware of the "truth" about *other lifetimes* and the *mysteries of the spiritual life*. In fact, I was even assured that I'd see him again in future lives. I was told that, no doubt, he and I had been in *several past lifetimes together* but not necessarily as father and son. Perhaps he was a friend, or perhaps I had been his father. This applied to *all* close relationships. Friends and family—we had all been together in previous lifetimes and would, no doubt, be together in the future ones, although not necessarily in the same relationship as this *present lifetime.*

My mind began reeling. It was sort of like walking in a very long, dark, narrow, and restrictive hallway when suddenly the walls on either side fall, full light is restored, and you can see forever in all directions. It doesn't take much to get a child's imagination rolling except this wasn't some imaginary thing. My mom said it; therefore, it must be true. I now had a purpose (at the age of seven!). I became devoted to my pursuit of learning about the "higher spiritual life" and was excited about going to the "next plane." If there was a next plane of existence, then I wanted to get on with it. In fact, on a number of occasions later in life (as a teenager), I actually contemplated suicide not due to any depression, anxiety, or despair but due *solely to my desire to learn more by getting to the next level.* Patience was never one of my strong suits. I finally stopped thinking about suicide when a Unity Sunday school teacher said that the only thing suicide would accomplish would be to *delay learning the lessons* this *particular incarnation* had in store for me and thus I'd have to start over in the next life. That settled it for me. Just as nobody wants to be held back to repeat a school year, I certainly didn't want to repeat a lifetime!

So my father died in February 1967; and as soon as the school year ended, we moved from Santa Cruz, California, to San Antonio, Texas. The cost of living in Texas was less than in California, and my uncle (my mother's brother) and his family lived in San Antonio. He was in the air force, which motivated me to enlist years later. My mother was a very strong and independent woman, but no matter how strong and independent a person might be, the sudden reality of being widowed with four young children takes its toll. She was happy to have her brother and his family close by. We got by on the social security payments we received since my father had served in the navy during World War II. Money was always tight. This seemed odd to me as the years went by because we were always practicing our "prosperity affirmations."

Meanwhile, as a newly transplanted seven-year-old, I found it very difficult to adjust to living in a new home and attending a new school. I was now in the second grade, and I cried nearly every day in school for the first week or so. I kept telling myself I'd get to see my dad again in the next life, but this couldn't keep me from all I was feeling. Eventually my crying stopped, and I settled in. Then came our first Christmas without our father. As difficult as that was, it was only made worse when we learned that year that Santa Claus didn't really exist. (Mom felt compelled to explain why there wouldn't be a lot of presents.) No comfort came from my dad this year. No comfort came from Santa either. Now this may not seem like much to you, dear reader, but when things you had relied on for your entire life are removed (even if that entire life only consists of seven years), it is pretty shattering. There's no Santa? Why did Mom lie to us about Santa Claus? Now there was nothing to get my hopes up at Christmas, and on top of all this, I no longer had a dad.

Then came hope. In addition to understanding reincarnation and being reunited at some point with my dad, there was another treasure to pin my aspirations on. I vividly recall being taught by my mother, Sunday school teachers, ministers, and the Unity books that we create our reality *by our thoughts*. This is a major tenet of the New Age, so I began a life of seeking to "create" a life. (I'll get to the New Age's nuts and bolts of creating a life in a moment.) So far, all I knew for sure was that after each life, we review our lives in preparation for reincarnating over and again. Next, I learned that we could actually control our lives by controlling our thoughts.

But there was more. I remember the first time I learned about *karma* (what the New Age terms "sowing and reaping"), and I remember it like it was yesterday. We were still in San Antonio, and I was sitting in the back seat of our family car on a trip. We had seen a fellow on the side of the road without any legs. I then remember overhearing my mother speaking with my aunt and uncle about *why* some people were born into poverty or with various deformities such as being born without legs, etc. According to Unity, it was due to the fact that in a previous life (or lives), the person had been guilty of egregious actions that resulted in the appropriate karmic effect being visited upon them. I remember crying convulsively. I had become terrified that in the next life, I might be born into misery because of what I had done in my previous lives. I was inconsolable, and this haunted me. But I was also told the karmic effect worked the other way too. By getting busy being positive, affirming only good things, helping others, practicing the principles of the New Age, doing good, and seeking to serve, I was actually *banking* some positive karma that would likewise pay off and could even reverse some of the bad stuff. Hope was restored along with my commitment to double down in the New Age. I could actually impact my own future lifetimes! I became zealous to reach the next level of spiritual growth. I was taught and believed in the old saying that I was "the master of my fate and the captain of my soul."

All these teachings come from the New Age and were strongly affirmed by my mother, so I accepted them without question 100 percent. And why not? Let's face it. If your parents taught you that *optometrists* and *lawyers* were evil, you would avoid any interactions with optometrists and lawyers. After all, *why would your parents lie?* It never occurred to me to ask my mother, "By what authority/evidence do you or Unity make these claims?" Every kid believes in Santa Claus for the same reason—somebody they respect and believe *told* them it was true, so it must be!

Let me also state that I don't hold my mother responsible here. She was doing what she thought was right. I remember her telling me how Unity helped her because she had grown up in a "strict Baptist church" that told her if she chewed gum or went to dances, she'd end up in hell. Of course, I wasn't there. I have no idea if that minister said that, nor do I know if my mother heard correctly. She had lots of stories like that. Apparently, it never occurred to her to read her Bible for herself because when I checked, there are no verses that tell someone they're going to hell for either dancing or chewing gum! I'm pretty sure anyone in that congregation who knew their Bibles either corrected that minister or left for a church that was obedient to the scriptures. Once again, we see the critical importance of my earlier question: Of the sum total of your Christian knowledge, what percentage of it is owing to what somebody *told you* the Bible said versus what you've *actually read, in context,* for yourself? All false religious teach so-called biblical views that hold countless souls in bondage because they simply believe in everything they're told, but they never search the scriptures to validate them, which the scriptures admonish us to do for that very reason.

My mother found Unity through a family friend, and due to its tremendous promises and appeal, she came to live and breathe it. She always had little signs and cards with positive affirmations and sayings posted around our home with the self-help "truths."

There were also helpful promptings to having a positive attitude, being persistent, etc. Those qualities help a person get out of bed in the morning, and there's nothing wrong with them. But there's a huge difference between having a good attitude, positive thinking, discipline, etc., and believing (as Unity and all New Age teaches) that you have the *power* to literally attract in your life *all your heart desires* (home, cars, yachts, relationships, etc.). At the same time, the New Age misses the point entirely of Jesus's words in Matthew 16:26, "For what profit is it to a man if he gains the whole world, and loses his own soul?" The New Age does not acknowledge heaven or hell other than as a "state of mind" that we are free to alter by exercising our "divine right" in ordering our thoughts to create the life we "so richly deserve."

After two years in San Antonio, the air force transferred my uncle and his family; and all of a sudden, we had a *family conference* that we were moving to El Paso. A longtime friend of my parents lived there, so we set off.

This was now the second time since my father's death that we'd move and I'd attend a new school and start over. I wasn't as devastated, though, because I was starting to grow up and learn how to adapt using the teachings of the New Age. My mother introduced me to a New Age booklet called *It Works.* This was a simple little pamphlet that made some terrific promises. It's still in print today, and here's a direct quote from the cover.

> *It Works* presents a concise, definite plan for bettering your conditions in life. It shows you how to

use the Mighty Power within that is anxious and
willing to serve you if you know how to use it.

This served to corroborate what I had been learning at Unity
all this time that you actually create your own reality. You have the
God-power within, and you are in control. Well, heck! Who would
say no to that? What could possibly be wrong with being empowered
(by the universe, no less) to visualize, claim, and receive whatever you
wanted?? How about *everything* is wrong with that!

As we'll see, the New Age points you completely away from
the reality of the Gospel of Christ. And how do they do this? First,
ignore the verses that don't agree with their teaching. Then reinterpret, misinterpret, twist, and spiritualize the Bible to say something
entirely different from what it says. Change and redefine (without
any authority at all, mind you) the words in the Bible (they do this by
using their own *Metaphysical Bible Dictionary*, which both redefines
and reassigns the biblical meaning of words). Furthermore, they deny
the existence of the very devil the Bible declares to be actual and true.

In the meantime, I felt so privileged to have this *great secret* of
manifesting my own happiness and circumstances. My positivity and
confidence began to soar. My hunger, passion, and desire to learn
about the spiritual realms; the "great law of cause and effect"; and
the how-tos of "claiming my rightful inheritance of health, wealth,
and prosperity" (as the New Age puts it) along with an awakening
of *channeling* and *astral travel* overcame me. (*Channeling* is when
one goes into a trance and *a being from another dimension* takes over
and communicates things from beyond. The person channeling, in
a trance, either speaks audibly or writes the things dictated by the
being[s] on the other side while communicating. There are many
books written [*Seth Speaks* comes to mind] where this phenomenon
is documented. *Astral projection* [also known as *soul flight*] is when
one has an out-of-body experience and travels to various spiritual
realms or various times.)

When I was older, I'd attend "past-life regression" sessions. This
is where I'd learn all about who I was and where I lived in previous
incarnations. I'd pay for personalized astrological charts that revealed

the meanings associated with my place and time of birth along with specific lessons laid out for me in this particular incarnation.

I was a voracious reader. We had many, many books by Unity authors as well as other New Thought writers, and I soon amassed a substantial personal library.

As far back as I could remember, our family would attend Sunday services at the local Unity Temple where we learned the "truth" about ourselves, the Bible, the afterlife, etc. In addition to being referred to as a Truth student, New Agers are often referred to as proponents of *New Thought* (this term was coined because "a new thought held in mind will always produce after its kind"). I continued New Age church attendance and practice right up until my Christian conversion many years later in 1991 at the age of thirty-one.

New Age Precepts

As stated earlier, New Agers refer to themselves as Truth students. They fully believe they have the higher truth when it comes to life, the afterlife, and how to be filled with health, wealth, and happiness. This is because of their firm stance in the area of metaphysics. *Metaphysics* is a word that means "the thought behind the physical," which may be summed up in a single sentence—"change your thoughts, change your life." This isn't a quaint saying; rather, it's a committed lifestyle, and they credit the Bible along with other Far East books and beliefs for their view. They believe that the Bible is the greatest and most deeply spiritual of all the scriptures; though they realize that other scriptures such as the Zend-Avesta and the Upanishads as well as the teaching of Buddha, the Koran, the Tao of Lao-tse, and the writings of Confucius contain expressions of eminent spiritual truths (*What Unity Teaches* 1952, 4).

The beauty of this belief system is that it puts you in charge and makes you your own god insofar as your life is concerned. You are the one in the cockpit and calling the shots. It's important to understand that the New Age teaches that we are "one with God." We are not God. I was taught this belief this way. Using our natural observation, we understand that the sun is the sun and always will be the sun. The sun is self-sustaining, bringing warmth and light, etc. The sun also shines beams of light. Each beam carries with it the essential properties of the sun itself. The beams are not the totality of the sun but rather are offshoots or manifestations of the sun. Then comes the connection. God (like the sun) is a self-sustaining principle. We, like the beams, are individualized sons of God that he forever emits. We now have the same properties as God. Therefore, since we read that God is love, *so then must man be.* In fact, because God is good, *everyone* born is good since everyone is one with God. Hence, man is born *good*. Man is noble and has the same creative abilities for his own individual life as God as for the universal life.

If you're scratching your head here, it's because you're not as "enlightened" as the rest of us who believed every word spilled from the pens of the great Unity writers. Here's a small sampling:

> Drop from your mind the belief that God is in any way separated from you, that He occupies form or space outside of you, or that he can be manifested to your consciousness in any except through your own soul. (Fillmore 1947, 27)

> God is not a person, having life, intelligence, love, power. God is that invisible, intangible, but very real something we call life. God is perfect love and infinite power. God is the total of these, the total of all good, whether manifested or unexpressed. (Cady 1944)

> To the individual consciousness God takes on personality, but as the creative underlying cause of all things, He is principle, impersonal; as expressed in each individual, He becomes personal to that one—a personal, loving, all-forgiving Father-Mother. All that we can ever need or desire is the infinite Father-Principle, the great reservoir of unexpressed good. There is no limit to the Source of our being, nor to His willingness to manifest more of Himself through us, when we are willing to His will. (Cady 1994, 11)

To further justify this, they'll quote Jesus's words from John 10:34, "Jesus answered them, 'Is it not written in your law, "I said, 'You are gods'"?'" Yet if anyone bothers to read the context as well as the Old Testament passages referred to it, things would clear up immediately. God had established judges to rule over his people, and their judgment was to be revered and obeyed since they were to reflect his judgment. They were referred to as gods (little *g*) because of their authority. Of course, later, God rebuked some of these judges who began taking bribes and ruling unjustly (see Ps. 82).

The name *Unity* was adopted in 1891 as "cofounder." Charles Fillmore stated, "To the spiritualization of humanity from an independent stand-point...a religion which took the best from all religions" (Freeman 1954, 55, 61). The New Age firmly believes and teaches that your very thoughts actually have the power to attract into your life everything you ever desired because you are literally the god of your life and creator of your own realities. And those thoughts are *attracting* things into your life whether you know it or not. Just as at the beginning of creation God said, "Let there be such and such, and it was so," we too can say, "Let there be something" and can expect its fulfillment. Why? Because man was created in God's image; thus, man is an individualized extension of God. God runs the macro-universe. We get to run our own micro-universe insofar as our personal lives are concerned.

Go to any self-help section of a bookstore, and the odds are that 100 percent of those books have some form of this view. All motivational books speak of the power of visualization, attraction, seeing it before it happens, naming and claiming it, etc. Probably one of the most popular books ever written on this subject would be Napoleon Hill's *Think and Grow Rich*, but it certainly isn't the only one. If you find yourself reading a book describing yourself as "pure consciousness" or using a capital "S" when referring to yourself, then beware: you are reading a book designed to draw you away from Christ as your Savior so that you rely on your own "self" righteousness.

The bottom line is that you are placed squarely on the throne of your own life, and I'm convinced that one of the reasons why New Agers are so happy and optimistic is because they feel in control. I know I sure did. Happy, positive thoughts equal a happy, positive life. Likewise, negative, unhappy thoughts equal a negative, unhappy life. And here's the best part. Since you can control your thoughts, you can control your life and everything in it (health, wealth, relationships, everything)! You can choose to be positive or negative, and *the universe will accommodate you* every time without fail. Again, let me state that there certainly isn't anything wrong with positive thinking. Let's face it. Most of us would prefer to be around someone positive and upbeat than a constantly negative person who's always dragging folks down. Of course, the only thing worse than optimism is false optimism. That is precisely what the New Age and all false religions provide—a system built upon falsehood and lies. It may be true that a person believes something to be true, but that doesn't mean that it *is* true. It only means they believe it and act accordingly.

Unity and New Age have an array of tools they prescribe to make sure you're creating only the life you want. Armed with the "truth" of creating my reality, my life became a series of "affirmation and denial" exercises as I sought to reprogram my subconscious into bringing me the life I wanted for myself. I began writing out my affirmations and denials hundreds and hundreds of times in my journals in an effort to reprogram my subconsciousness. I'll explain how all this works in a bit.

Of course, if it *doesn't* "work," we're told that we are either (1) clearly *not* believing or programming diligently enough (your faith is weak) or (2) that due to the enormity of the negative seeds (accumulated through thousands or perhaps *millions* of lifetimes), we must power-through with greater fervency and ferocity knowing that eventually the results will (ay, must!) manifest themselves. It's sort of like the farmer having to turn up the clods on very dry and rocky soil in order to prepare it. And how can I be certain of this? "Why, just look at nature," they'd say! Just as surely as the literal ground produces the seeds implanted upon it with proper preparation, etc., so too does our spiritual subconscious mind respond to the seeds consciously implanted into it.

This was my life until God rescued me. Until that moment of being born again, I was a steadily devoted practitioner of the New Age because it was all I knew. I was 100 percent *positive* I was on the right track all along. This was spoon-fed to me from as far back as I can remember. *Hey, if Mom says it's true, then it must be, right?* And best of all, I was assured that much of their teachings came directly from the Bible itself, a book nearly all hold in high esteem. But did those teachings really come from the Bible? Well, yes and no; that is, the Bible actually has the words and verses that are quoted, but the New Age *assigns not only different meanings* to those words but also *believes it has perfect immunity* in "spiritualizing" the text. This means they can make it say whatever fits into the New Age presuppositions. In the original *Wizard of Oz* series of books written by L. Frank Baum (May 15, 1856–May 6, 1919), green-tinted spectacles were handed out to everyone entering the Emerald City. In this way, everything became green-tinted. Of course, *nothing* was actually green-tinted, which could be proved as soon as somebody removed the spectacles. But as long as they had them on, everything was green. This is what the New Age does. When it comes to reading and understanding your Bible, *they hand you a set of spectacles* (which is their "take" on the Holy Scriptures) and thereby assure your conclusions will be in accordance with their beliefs and *not what the Bible actually says*.

Here's How It Works

Are you ready to hear how you can *think* and *grow rich*? How you can "name it and claim it" and enjoy that life you're entitled to? How to enjoy countless lives of peace, joy, and plenty? Here's how I was taught it. Before going any further, let me say that the Bible *does not* support this one iota. In fact, the Bible has a lot to say about the horrific minefield this entire doctrine creates. Contrary to the beliefs of millions or even billions of sincere souls, life is *not* about cultivating your awareness of the "God spark" within you or achieving cosmic consciousness and thus overcoming the necessity of reincarnations. I'll cover the problem with the New Age and Unity in a later chapter.

Mind you, I did not know what the Bible said at the time. I only knew what my teachers *told* me it said, but clearly they didn't know what it says either. They didn't know because they were steeped in blindness and ignorance as is everyone who isn't born again and regenerated by the Spirit of God. I know that sounds offensive. You've heard the saying "nothing personal, it's business." Likewise, when it comes to their biblical ignorance, it's "nothing personal, it's *spiritual.*" First Corinthians 2:14 declares, "The natural man does not receive the things of the Spirit of God, for they are foolishness to him; *nor can he know them* [italics added], because they are spiritually discerned." The Bible distinguishes between the *natural man* (the condition of original sin we are all born with) and the *spiritual man* (the state of the regenerated, born-again soul).

Furthermore, this verse declares that the things of God are foolish to the natural man and that he *cannot* know them. There's a difference between *can* not and *may* not. *Can* implies "ability." *May* implies "permission." The natural man has *permission* to read the Bible but does have the *ability* to know the truth without being born again by the Spirit of God. The Bible tells us there is blindness in the unregenerate man whose understanding is covered by a veil. Second Corinthians 3:16 says, "Nevertheless when one turns to the Lord, the veil is taken away." This is why 1 Corinthians 1:18–19 declares, "The message of the cross is foolishness to those who are perishing, but to us who are being saved it is the power of God."

Here's how the New Age explains their doctrine of cause and effect.

Think of a very rich and fertile field. That field will produce for you whatever is planted, whether roses, vegetables, fruit trees, or weeds. The field always says yes to whatever is planted. *It doesn't ask questions or give opinions.* Its job is to grow things using the laws of nature.

Now think of the seed that is to be planted in that field. The seed can be large or small. The seed, once buried into that field under the correct conditions, *will* sprout and bring forth whatever it is. But *only* that seed will sprout. No seed, no sprout. Good seed, good sprout. Bad seed, bad sprout. It doesn't matter to the ground.

Get the picture? Now watch this. In the New Age, we're taught that the *conscious mind* contains the seed-thoughts that we sow. These seeds are your conscious thoughts, ideals, desires, and goals. They are the things and conditions you desire to "manifest," express, and show forth in your life. The seeds are limitless. The *subconscious mind* is the fertile ground. The subconscious *always* says yes. And just as when the natural seed is planted, the laws of nature work to bring it forth so the subconscious mind accepts the seed planted by the conscious mind and will *always* bring forth whatever is held in mind. Read that again. Furthermore, it can *only* bring forth what you've planted. You'll never get an apple tree from an orange seed. You can swear up and down all day that you planted an apple tree, but if an orange tree grows, then we can know for certain you were mistaken. Knowingly or unknowingly, you clearly planted an orange seed. It's simply impossible that anything other than an orange could grow there.

You say, "What's your point?" Just this—according to New Thought and New Age beliefs, your life *only* produces what you've planted, whether knowingly or unknowingly. If your life is *not* producing health, wealth, and happiness, then it's because *you* didn't plant the correct seeds. If your life is demonstrating poor health, lack, etc., then it's *only* because *those* seeds have been planted; and because *the laws of nature are unfailing*, you are reaping the crop you've sown. "Oh, but I *am* thinking those positive thoughts," you'd say. The New Age reply is "Apparently *not sufficiently enough* to supplant and uproot the existing crop. Otherwise, that is what would be manifesting."

Another convenient reply is to point out that since you've now awakened to the "truth" of your cosmic abilities (this is their definition of the biblical mandate of being *born again*), you "obviously" have much negative thinking to undo and reverse from what's been accumulated for possibly several hundred or millions of lifetimes. Therefore, persist and stick to it, and it *will* turn around. Imagine a pitcher with water swirling vigorously in one direction. Now imagine putting a large spoon into the swirling water as you begin to stir it in the *opposite* direction. The initial result is chaos, but eventually it all turns around. Thus, we again prove the law of cause and effect. (Get used to that term. When they refer to the "law" of cause and effect, it is a law that always operates like the laws of mathematics.)

Here are the two most popular tools the New Age uses to reprogram the subconscious mind to reap the "healthy, happy life we all deserve." They are *affirmations and denials* and *treasure-mapping*:

1. *Affirmations and denials.* This is where you either affirm a truth ("I am healthy, happy, and whole.") or deny a negative trait you wish to eliminate ("I refuse to believe in the power of disease."). This is a must and has to be done each and every day in order for the subconscious to accept it. These are typically written, silently meditated upon, and spoken aloud over and over. Sometimes an affirmation and denial are paired together. Myrtle Fillmore claims her healing came about as she affirmed, "I am a child of God and therefore do not inherit sickness." Unity insists it is the *habitual and specific planting* (affirmations) and weeding (denials) of our mental garden that yields the results we

long for. It's an Aladdin's lamp promising to grant unlimited wishes.

2. *Treasure-mapping.* This is where you take a poster board and place a picture of yourself in the center (or you would draw a circle and write, "The Christ of Me"). You then cut out magazine pictures and images of things that represent the things you wish to attract and place them around your image. The pictures can be of anything—a bigger/nicer car, a house, the perfect mate/spouse, career, etc. You place this poster in a place where you'll see it every day, deliberately imagining (and *feeling*) yourself actually possessing whatever images you're looking at. Why? In order to feed and plant your subconsciousness. By gazing upon these images, you are imprinting your subconscious mind (that always says yes).

Other ways to program your mind are guided meditations, hypnosis, and even *subliminal recordings.* I purchased recordings of ocean waves that supposedly contained subliminal autosuggestions of health, wealth, and happiness that would *feed directly* into the subconscious mind, bypassing any barrier, interference, or reluctance my conscious mind might be creating. You could find subliminal recordings to stop smoking, drinking, and remove your cancer; the selections were limitless. We were told the primary benefit to these autosuggestion recordings was how they could plant those seeds of positivity, health, abundance, etc., *without the hindrance of conscious doubts* that might be lurking about to choke it and keep it from sprouting.

This is exciting stuff because it puts *you* in the cockpit. And what keeps it all alive? Why, the law of cause and effect, of course—a law that is universal and works always!

Having fully accepted this (and having been assured that this was all biblically based), I believed and practiced wholeheartedly all that I learned from Unity and other teachings of the New Age.

Remember, the theme is that we all have that "God-spark" within us (this is their definition of Christ) and are masters of our own destinies by choosing our thoughts.

Where do they come up with this explanation? Why, by arbitrarily putting it into the *Metaphysical Bible Dictionary!* Prior to my salvation, I didn't realize that the Bible holds to the reality that Jesus Christ is God Almighty in the flesh (John 1:1, 14; Phil. 2:6,7). But Unity, with *absolutely no authority* whatsoever to change Holy Writ, presents a different view.

> Christ, meaning "messiah" or "anointed," designates one who had received a spiritual quickening from God, while Jesus is the name of the personality. To the metaphysical Christian—that is, to him who studies the spiritual man—Christ is the name of the super mind and Jesus is the name of the personal consciousness. The spiritual man is God's Son; the personal man is man's son. (Fillmore 1947, 10)

It's important to keep elevating your *consciousness*. Their definition of consciousness is "the conscious awareness of who you are." You will *always* and *only* manifest your consciousness—cause and effect.

The New Age would have you believe that you're the king and the universe is your cosmic bellhop that only *wants* to serve you. The universe is the great benevolent power of "divine love" that seeks to bless you in giving you all that you ardently desire.

I can still remember one of my favorite Sunday school teachers saying how these truths were the "greatest do-it-yourself projects of all time!" I was actually *in control* of my own destiny! I could affirm all the prosperity I wanted. I could deny all the negative things away too.

I was at a conference where a person told the story of how he had been healed from a health ailment using the power of affirmation. He had been given an affirmation by his minister with the promise that it would "lay claim" to his deserved healing. He was to repeat his affirmation daily in a prescribed manner until he manifested it. This particular affirmation was evidently long and difficult to remember. "I just couldn't remember what I was supposed to say!" he continued. "I got so frustrated that I just blurted out to the universe, 'Oh hell, I'm well!'" The place erupted in laughter. He was so pleased as he reported that his health had returned. I was taught that although he didn't use his affirmation word for word, it was the thought that actually counted. This is known as touching the hem of the garment. In the Bible (Matt. 9), there was a woman suffering for years a severe health ailment and wanted an audience with Jesus for healing. Although a crowd thronged around him, she determined that if she could *only touch the hem of his garment*, she'd be healed. That is exactly what happened. So in the New Age, even if you don't precisely have the consciousness you're looking for, if you can at the very least reach it *with a mustard seed of faith* and 'touch the hem,'" the healing would take effect.

Knowing then that your thoughts manifest themselves, you must be very guarded in what you think. This means affirming only good things and immediately denying anything negative lest it take root. When I was nineteen years old and in the air force, we were told that we all had to have our flu shots. Mind you, to the New Ager, the flu (like anything else) is subject to *us* and not the other way around. I remember hearing a woman in the office (who was also a New Ager) vehemently refusing to take her shot, proudly declaring, "I don't do the flu!" Many laughed and mocked, but I knew exactly what she was doing. She was using her affirmations to keep her subconscious mind from sprouting the flu!

I also began noticing New Age concepts in music and films and television. I remember a particular episode from the original *Star Trek* television series. The crew visited a planet in which *whatever you thought about* became real. (Does that sound familiar?) If a member of the crew thought about a lost loved one, they'd appear! Likewise, if they thought about war or an enemy, etc., then that would appear as well. As you can imagine, this planet was beautiful and terrifying at the same time, limited *only* by the thoughts of the one thinking them. The crew was encouraged to a respite on the planet, provided they took special care over their thought-life. Ironically, that episode aired on December 29, 1966. I was six years old and only two months away from losing my father. I saw it later in a rerun. You can imagine the impact this episode had on me. I knew that *Star Trek* was a fictional show. Nevertheless, that episode served to reiterate how we all must choose our thoughts carefully because those thoughts, once planted, *will sprout*. It was the same thing years later when the first *Star Wars* movie came out. I immediately picked up on the Force, an incredible power that could be wielded for either *good* or *evil*. The Force was completely compliant, subject only to the thoughts and desires of the one using it. And I was assured it was entirely biblical.

This just proved to me that I was on the right track. Since I had never studied my Bible, I had no way of understanding verses such as 1 John 5:19, "We know that we are of God, *and the whole world lies under the sway of the wicked one* [italics added]." If you don't believe there's a devil, you have no reason to think you're being duped! As a New Ager, I was told that there was no "wicked one" or, for that matter, that neither God nor the devil were actual personal beings but rather were principles of light and dark. We had all the power and could use it for our betterment or detriment, but *we* decided. I had no idea of the true story of creation, the fall of man, the consequences of that fall, redemption, the substitutionary atonement for sin, salvation, damnation, etc.

I recall a particular affirmation that Unity taught called the Prayer of Protection that one would say anytime they left their homes or traveled or whatever. It goes like this, "The light of God surrounds me. The love of God enfolds me. The power of God protects me. And the presence of God watches over me. Wherever I am, God is."

For *years*, that little affirmation served me the way the Linus blanket served him. I must have said that affirmation thousands of times. It was my mantra, spoken multiple times daily for many years.

There are other New Age techniques, but the basic principle is "Change your thoughts, change your life." I realize all of this sounds harmless, but it has absolutely *no* basis in reality whatsoever. Nor does the Bible teach this (even though I was assured over and again that it did). Let me state again that there's nothing wrong with preferring to be positive. A positive attitude is something very helpful. It inspires confidence. But when you form a biblical doctrine that states that your thoughts are the ones actually controlling the circumstances, it's a bridge too far.

What the New Age does (as do all false religions) is what's known as *prooftexting*. You begin with a premise and then try to find verses to fit that premise. Rather than the Bible saying what it means and meaning what it says, the New Age would have you start with the Bible meaning what *they* say and saying what *they* mean. The New Age loves to take a verse completely out of context to support a claim even though the falsity of their beliefs is proven over and again by the Bible itself.

Allow me to prove how anyone can make the Bible say whatever they want it to say. Did you know that both Psalm 14 and 53 state that *there is no God*? It says those words very clearly and explicitly, "There is no God." That is an irrefutable, scriptural *fact*. But what happens when you read those words in context? Here is the entire verse quoted from Psalm 14:1 (which is quoted verbatim again in Psalm 53:1), "The fool has said in his heart, 'There is no God.' They are corrupt, they have done abominable works, there is none who does good."

How about that? It turns out the Bible *does* say, "There is no God." But when you read those words in context, everything changes, doesn't it? It says that the *fool* says in his heart, "There is no God."

The New Age teaches the Bible is open to many interpretations. And why not? To a New Ager, it's not meant to be taken literally but rather allegorized and spiritualized so the true meaning is completely obfuscated from its original intent. This is a very convenient way to avoid being held accountable.

Here's the problem with misplaced faith.

Faith means belief. Everyone exercises faith. Every time you sit in a chair, you exercise faith that the chair is going to hold you up. But what if your faith is misplaced? What if you have all the faith in the world in something that simply isn't true?

Unity teaches that the Bible, while considered as their "basic textbook," must nevertheless be interpreted metaphysically and not literally.

Unity provided me with a copy of the *Metaphysical Bible Dictionary* that *redefines* biblical words to fit the New Age narrative. Whenever I'd come upon words such as *law, heaven, hell, sin,* or *Christ* in my Bible, I'd stop and look up their definition in my *Metaphysical Bible Dictionary.* How dangerous is that? How about *extremely* dangerous! This is the same as someone giving you a perfectly functioning compass and telling you that the key to using it correctly is to remember that the needle *always* points *south.* And so you confidently set out with a perfectly working compass, but your instruction in its use is incorrect and false. Nevertheless, you've been told the needle always points south by someone you trust. So you set out on your journey armed with your new compass and instruction. What could go wrong? The problem is the needle, in fact, points *north*! This isn't open to interpretation. It's a fact. How does this affect your journey, then? Let this next sentence set in. It means that literally *every* decision you make with this compass will be *wrong* 100 percent of the time because you're using it incorrectly!

It's not the compass's fault. The problem arises when the compass is *misused.* This is precisely the quagmire my *Metaphysical Bible Dictionary* placed me in. Mind you, I already had a Bible (in fact, Unity *gave* me a Bible). It's a real Bible too. But I also had my *Metaphysical Bible Dictionary* codebook to help me understand the Bible. When they change the meaning of the words, it changes everything. The words are the same for everybody, but not everybody is treating those words in the same way.

For instance, according to the *Metaphysical Bible Dictionary, Christ* means "the divine spark within all of us." You read that right. Here's the direct quote from their *Metaphysical Bible Dictionary.*

> Christ is the only begotten Son of God, the one complete idea or perfect man and divine Mind. This Christ or perfect-man idea existing eternally in divine Mind is the true, spiritual, *higher-self of every individual.* (*Metaphysical Bible Dictionary,* 150; italics added)

Unity distinguishes between Jesus and the Christ.

> The difference between Jesus and us is not one
> of inherent spiritual capacity, but in difference of
> demonstration of it. Jesus was potentially perfect,
> and we have not yet expressed it. (*What Unity
> Teaches*, 5)

So you see, according to the New Age, we all have this higher
self indwelling us and only need to fan the flame for it to find full
expression as Jesus did. Those of you who know your Bibles know
fully well that this is a completely fabricated tale with only one intention—*to lead you away from the only hope for the salvation of your soul.*

The New Age teaches that man is basically good since he is a
light beam of God. That "divine spark" is in all of us, and our biggest
problem is rediscovering the truth so we can live effective lives by
utilizing this spark for ourselves and others. Is that what the Bible
says, that man is basically good and a light beam of God? No, dear
reader, not at all.

Furthermore, I was taught that the definition of *sin* was "a sense
of separation from this divine spark." We are told that it is by accepting this erroneous view that we are separated from our indwelling
good that causes our subconscious to produce this as our reality, creating lack and disease. The remedy is to "repent" (change your thinking that you are separate from your God-spark) and begin embracing
the "truth" so you can demonstrate the health, wealth, and happiness
you deserve. We "repent" of this "error" by affirmations and denials
to wit.

> Pain, sickness, poverty, old age and death are not
> real and they no power over me. There is noth-
> ing in all the universe for me to fear. (*Lessons in
> Truth*, 35)

> 1. I deny that I have inherited disease, sick-
>   ness, ignorance or any mental limitation

whatsoever. 2. I deny that I am child of the flesh. I deny all belief in evil, for God made all that really is and pronounced it good. 3. Therefore no such deception as a belief in evil can darken my clear understanding of Truth. 4. I deny that the sins and omissions of my ancestors can reflect upon me in any way. Selfishness, envy, malice, jealousy, pride, arrogance, cruelty, hypocrisy, obstinacy and revenge are not part of my present understanding and I deny all such beliefs. (Fillmore 1942, 250–251)

My friend, before I was saved by the grace of God and before I read the Bible for myself *without* their "metaphysical spectacles," I fully *agreed with every word* taught by the Unity (and all New Age) authors.

But now that my eyes have been opened to the truth of the scriptures, I am both *embarrassed* and *thankful*—embarrassed that for thirty-one years, I accepted without question this wholly *unscriptural* and *unauthorized view*. Once more, I must ask: With what authority do they so boldly and flippantly change or add to the Holy Scriptures, *especially in light of specific warnings against doing so*? For Unity to state on one hand to hold the Holy Bible in high esteem and then on the other hand *deny* the very doctrines within the Bible is untenable and damnable. Every one of the statements in the previous quotes is directly and clearly refuted in the Bible. This is the height of haughtiness to redefine then erroneously proclaim the teachings the Word of God so clearly refutes. This is akin to a Truth student standing in the path of a giant roaring tidal wave while shaking his fist arrogantly and proclaiming in his "enlightenment," "I do not believe in this erroneous idea of moisture. Therefore, it has no power over me." A split second later, he is *drenched*.

Let me state again that everyone is entitled to their opinions. But this is more than mere opinion. The New Age is teaching as "truth" their "higher knowledge from the metaphysical and spiritual

36

interpretations of the Bible." *To claim to know* and then pollute millions upon millions of lost souls with these damnable lies is to be the effective tool of the devil himself, and the tragedy is that all the while they are doing the bidding of the devil, they don't acknowledge his reality of being. Rightly did our Lord say of false teachers, "Every plant which My heavenly Father has not planted will be uprooted. Let them alone. They are blind leaders of the blind. And if the blind leads the blind, both will fall into a ditch" (Matt. 15:13–14).

In addition to being embarrassed at these false statements, I was also so very *thankful* to have been rescued from a lifetime of lies, bondage, and misplaced faith and hope. As Scripture puts it, "If you abide in My word, you are My disciples indeed. And you shall *know the truth*, and *the truth shall make you free*" (John 8:31–32; italics added). I am now the recipient of the distinguished grace of God "who loved me and gave Himself for me" (Gal. 2:20).

And you shall know *the truth*—the truth as it revealed in the Bible, not as it is twisted to accommodate man's depraved desire to sit on the throne of his own life as though he were God (as fully expressed in their *Metaphysical Bible Dictionary* and all other New Age writings).

Dear reader, the cunning manipulators are in the New Age. So well did the apostle Paul write in 1 Corinthians 3:19, "For the wisdom of this world is foolishness with God," and Colossians 2:8, "Beware lest anyone cheat you through philosophy and empty deceit, according to the tradition of men, according to the basic principles of the world, and not according to Christ."

The New Age promises nothing but success. This is cruel. This fosters not only a false hope but also further steeps the New Age adherent deeper and deeper into darkness and ultimately, if not repented of, eternal damnation.

And here's yet another problem this false teaching begets. Whether we want to admit it or not, many of us lie to ourselves. It's part and parcel of our fallen nature. Take the person who is addicted to buying via credit. "I'll pay for it in the future and I can have what I want now," they say. Of course, when the "future" comes, the person is still living in the "present;" and in addition to dealing with this "present" financial situation, he also now has to deal with his past purchase that caused the current financial situation to boot. It's so easy for people to fall headlong into credit debt due to lack of discipline, foresight and, quite frankly, lying to themselves that it will all somehow work out. Now let's change lanes and apply this to the spiritual realm. When a person knows they have multiple lifetimes to work out their "karmic debt" of bad choices, it becomes easy to justify your actions into thinking you can deal with it "tomorrow" even if tomorrow is over several lifetimes. Perhaps you're rolling your eyes right now, asking, "Who would be so foolish as to put such stumbling blocks in a future life?" My answer is the same people who allow their credit card to control them instead of vice versa. And by the way, I myself actually had those thoughts; and I'm quite sure others did too.

You can tell a lot about a person by glancing at their personal library. Whenever I'd attend an estate sale, it would always break my heart to come across book titles such as *How to Heal Your Body of Cancer*, etc., or books that promote any kind of self-healing. And when the people die since they did *not* heal themselves of cancer (or whatever it was), we're conveniently told, "It was their time to graduate and move on."

How often do you hear people say to those in difficulty that they're sending them "good thoughts," "positive vibrations," or "creative visualizations" with the hopes of some sort of deliverance? My friends, there is nothing in the Bible that supports this. Of course, the Bible *does* say that we make our requests known directly to the Almighty God. Prayer is effective because the Bible says it's effective. But the bottom line is in all prayer, they must always be prefaced with "If it is your will." Something to keep in mind—*God alone has all power*. God isn't just powerful. He has *all* the power. God alone runs our lives and the universe. He is intimately acquainted with all. And because he is eternal and infinite, he is able to stay 100 percent present in our lives 100 percent of the time. This means you are *never* without the presence of God Almighty. But I'm speaking of the God of the Bible—the God of Abraham, Isaac, and Jacob—not the New Age god who is a "life principle" and a "loving Father-Mother" force. According to Unity, "The Father is Principle, The Son is that Principle revealed in the creative plan, the Holy Spirit is the executive power of both Father and Son carrying out the plan" (*Metaphysical Bible Dictionary*, 629). God is "principle"? Where, pray tell, is God (and any of the Trinity) revealed in the Holy Scriptures as principle?

So now we know how Unity and the New Age (who supposedly revere the scriptures) define God. Let's see how the Bible *itself* defines God. The late great Dr. Walter Martin wrote:

> Scripture teaches very clearly that God is personal spirit possessed of attributes which only a personality has, immanent in creation, but apart from it as Creator. Transcendent in that He does not share His spiritual substance (John 4:24; Hebrews 1:3) with the products of His creative will.
>
> A. God remembers. Isaiah 43:25; Jeremiah 31:20; Hosea 8:13.
> B. God speaks. (Subject-object relationship). Exodus 3:12, Matthew 3:17; Luke 17:6.
> C. God sees, hears, and creates. Genesis 6:5; Exodus 2:24, Genesis 1:1
> D. God knows (has a mind). Jeremiah 29:11; 2 Timothy 2:19, 1 John 2:17.
> E. God is a personal spirit. John 4:24; Hebrews 1:3
> F. God has a will. Matthew 6:10; Hebre3ws 19:7, 9; 1 John 23:17.
> G. God will judge. Ezekiel 18:30; 34:20; 2 Corinthians 5:10. (Martin 1968, 295–296)

Again, we see that Unity's (and all the New Age's) explanations fall far short of what the Bible actually declares. The Bible itself refutes their metaphysical interpretations. Knowing what the Bible says, how could anyone *think otherwise*? Simple! Those who are blinded and under the sway of the enemy of their souls, the devil, are easily swayed. I sure was.

Today, if someone asks me to pray for another's affliction with, say, alcoholism or some other addiction, I'm happy to do so. But the first thing I always ask is whether or not the person we're praying for is saved. Have they come to Christ? After all, it does nobody any good *to be completely clean and sober yet still perish in hell.*

Unity teaches that *we* are to atone for ourselves by using the mighty power within.

> We have thought that we are to be saved by Jesus' making personal petitions and sacrifices for us, but now we see that are to be saved by using the creative principles that he developed in Himself and that is ever ready to cooperate with us in developing in ourselves by observing the law has He observed it. "In them, and thou in me, that they may be perfected into one." (*Jesus Christ Heals*, 162)

Wasn't that a nice touch—the way he quoted a partial scripture there at the end? Reader, if you have no idea what the Bible says, you could well be susceptible to accepting that quote. I can assure you that quote could not be farther from the truth!

Of course, we are saved by Jesus's personal sacrifice and petition. How do I know? Because the Bible expressly declares this! This is precisely why Jesus came (we don't need to metaphysically interpret anything else to the contrary)!

> The Son of Man did not come to be served, but to serve, and to give His life a ransom for many. (Mark 10:45)

> For there is one God and one Mediator between God and men, the Man Christ Jesus, who gave Himself a ransom for all. (1 Tim 2:5–6)

They teach that Jesus was the individual personality who finally became the Christ as he "embraced the reality of that God-spark within him." There are beliefs in the New Age that Jesus was actually an allegorical fiction and not a historical figure.

How does this "sin" affect the New Ager? If you believe you are separated and cut off from the Great I Am and the mighty power within, your subconscious *goes to work* to bring lack, poverty, illness, etc. It's like a branch that believes he's separated from the tree. He denies himself the opportunity to bear fruit. This wrong thinking can only be remedied by changing one's thoughts and mind (their definition of *repentance*) to accepting the truth of this divine spark, and all will be well.

"Where do they get that definition of sin?" you might ask. They sure don't get it from the Bible. There's no ambiguity. No matter how badly one wants to spiritualize a text, you cannot deny that the Bible clearly defines sin.

> Whoever commits sin also commits lawlessness,
> and sin is lawlessness. (1 John 3:4)

Breaking God's law (whether not doing what he commands or doing what he forbids) is sin. This verse makes it crystal clear that sin has nothing to do with one's own "sense of separation from God" but rather one's disobedience *to* God.

"Change your thoughts, change your life" is the mantra of all New Age thinking and practice, which I accepted and pursued completely in all things. Of course, *there's no biblical authority* to prove any of this except for the verses Unity conveniently takes out of context and *plenty* of scriptures to refute it.

I was ten or eleven when a Sunday school teacher impressed upon me the belief that *we attract our circumstances by the very power of our thoughts*, whether for our good or our hurt, since we alone control those thoughts.

She took a partial verse from the Old Testament book of Job. In Job 3:25, Job says (after profound calamities had befallen him), "The thing I greatly feared has come upon me and what I dreaded has happened to me." This was our proof! Here's a fellow named Job who experienced gut-wrenching losses and dire circumstances and came to the conclusion that it all happened because of his fearful thoughts that manifested themselves in his life.

My teacher expounded the false New Age doctrine that the *only* reason Job experienced the ruin he did was that *he had been thinking negatively* and thus "manifested" that which he dwelled upon. In fact, he *must* "demonstrate" this experience because (here comes the lie!) *we only experience what we first attract through our all-powerful thoughts*; that is, *our effect* is *only* and *always* whatever *our cause* is, set in motion through our conscious thoughts. Thus, Job's subconscious properly responded by bringing to fruition those thoughts to his great demise and grief and horror. After all, doesn't the Bible teach that Job said, "The thing I greatly feared has come upon me and what I dreaded has happened to me"?

Dear reader, this terrified me because I was now being shown how our thoughts really *do* control our lives. Good thoughts equal good life. Bad or evil equals "watch out!" And it was right out of the Bible! I must now vigilantly guard my thought life to think positively and outright reject any negativity whatsoever. This rejecting of negativity is also known as the "rising above it" in our consciousness. I now had a biblical truth to stand on that my thoughts (and my thoughts alone) would plant either positive or negative seeds into my subconscious mind, which had no choice but to grow and develop those seeds.

It wasn't until after my conversion all those years later that while reading Job, I recognized how that verse had been misapplied to teach something that fits their narrative. Even a cursory reading of the first two chapters of the book of Job would *eliminate* that cause-effect concept entirely. Job's thoughts (good or bad) had *nothing* to do with the afflictions that came upon him, nor did it have anything to do with what followed. If I had just read those first two chapters back when I was ten! What was the bottom line? It is yet another proof that Unity and the evil New Age had *lied, misrepresented,* and *misled.* It's a trick employed by the devil over and again—misrepresent, flatter, assure that you're on the right track, etc. But I must state again. How on earth could I have known that? I didn't read my Bible (except with my great codebook). I accepted and believed whatever I was told *about* my Bible.

Ironically, it's that same Bible that says that when it comes to spiritual matters and doctrine, we are to "test all things" (1 Thess. 5:21); and 1 John 4:1–2 declares, "Beloved, do not believe every spirit, *but test the spirits, whether they are of God* [italics added]; because many false prophets have gone out into the world." The Bereans themselves were highly commended in the scriptures for one reason. It was because they "received the word with all readiness, and searched the Scriptures daily to find out whether these things were so" (Acts 17:11). The greatest commentary on the Bible *is* the Bible itself, *not* anyone's interpretation of it.

Unity, Christian Science, Science of the Mind, and most other New Age organizations freely quote the Bible in their literature. This gives them a semblance of legitimacy as well as a nonthreatening "Christian appeal." A person who was dissatisfied with their current church experience, such as my mother, is easily wooed to this freeing new "theology" and "truth" since it uses the same Bible and words and passages one is familiar with. They put a metaphysical spin on it; thus, they change its meaning entirely. This is the problem with a half-truth. It is mixed with a lie and just enough to become believable. The verses *are* from the Holy Bible, but the twisted and misleading understanding of those verses is from the devil. Religions that boast having a "spiritual interpretation of the scriptures" or hidden keys to understanding the great secrets of the universe sounds good, doesn't it? It makes you feel as though you were able to break away from the masses and find your own secret path. But the Bible, God's Word, tells us that *it* is our authority as is. All those who are downtrodden and looking for salvation are welcome.

> My soul faints for Your salvation, but I hope in
> *Your word*. (Ps. 119:81; italics added)

Whenever someone would challenge my views with a Bible verse, I'd have the perfect pat answer, "That's just *your* interpretation of the Bible, and everyone knows there are many interpretations. Furthermore, the Bible was written by men who all wanted to make their own points. It has been rewritten and translated over and over throughout history. There are so many things that were lost over the years. That's why we use the Bible, but it's only *one* source of truth."

That's a pretty swift dodge, isn't it? It sure served me well. I stopped many arguments dead on its tracks with that logic. Of course, *I had never read the entire Bible for myself*. I really didn't need to. I had spiritual teachers who told me what it said, what to think, and how to understand it once it's *metaphysically interpreted*. Some of you will agree with this line of thinking. You can't help it. But those who know their Bibles will readily recognize this as one of the greatest of lies all cults and false religions love to employ. Furthermore, the Bible itself destroys these arguments.

Unity ignores the verses that destroy that pat answer such as the following:

- "No prophecy of Scripture is of any private interpretation, for prophecy never came by the will of man, but holy men of God spoke as they were moved by the Holy Spirit" (2 Pet. 1:20–21).
- "All Scripture is given by inspiration of God, and is profitable for doctrine, for reproof, for correction, for instruction in righteousness, that the man of God may be complete, thoroughly equipped for every good work" (2 Tim. 3:16–17).
- "Every word of God is pure; He is a shield to those who put their trust in Him. Do not add to His words, lest He rebuke you, and you be found a liar" (Prov. 30:5–6).

To begin with, the Bible means what it says and says what it means. The Bible defines sin as disobeying God. First John 3:4 says, "Whoever commits sin also commits lawlessness, and sin is lawlessness."

Sin is *not* suffering from a "sense of separation from the Great I am and the mighty power within."

44

New Agers love to point out that the word *sin* is an old archery term that quite literally means "missing the mark." When an archer shot his arrow and the arrow fell short, he sinned. The New Age says that when we "miss the mark" of the "truth" of who we are and thus manifest that erroneous idea, we are sinning.

But that's *not* the way the Bible uses the word. We're missing the mark all right—but that mark is the perfect righteousness which God requires. It is "to flat-out disobey God." It is not only doing what God forbids, but it is also failing to do what God commands. Why should this matter? Because contrary to what the New Age teaches about God, the Bible declares a number of things that are extremely uncomfortable. Yes, God is love, patient, merciful, and gracious. But the Bible also declares, "Our God is a consuming fire" (Heb. 12:29), and "It is a fearful thing to fall into the hands of the living God" (Heb. 10:31). The Bible states quite plainly that the wages of sin is death (Rom. 6:23).

"Wait! That's just *your* interpretation!" is the common protest. Really? Well, how would *you* interpret those verses differently unless you were using their codebook?

All the while, Unity produced conferences, books, publications, and pamphlets confirming that these truths were, in fact, true while using many biblical verses to "support" them. Every Sunday, I'd be surrounded by other Truth students who also affirmed them. Because I had never actually read the Bible, how was I to know that Unity was doing the very thing the Bible warns against?

Another objection New Ager's use is that they use the Bible as just one of many books. But let's get down to brass tacks. When you sum up all New Age (and false religious cult) doctrines, you will find that it is *antibiblical every time*; that is, it says precisely the opposite or is against what the Bible actually says.

My Life as a New Ager

I became quite the New Age evangelist even in grade school because I was the funny, positive, and confident kid who could tell the other kids *the secret of getting whatever they wanted.*

Every now and then throughout my childhood and teen years, I'd run into those pesky born-again Christians who'd refute my beliefs, and all I had to say was "Well, that's just *your* interpretation. All spiritual things can be seen literally or metaphysically or spiritually, and you're simply choosing to dwell on the literal one." I hadn't yet run into any who had a grasp on their Bibles, which would have easily unarmed me.

I recall times when friends and school acquaintances told me about hell and how Jesus saves. I didn't like being told I was bad. I didn't like being told I was going to hell, but not for the reasons most don't like being told that. I didn't like it because it didn't line up with everything my mother and religion in Unity taught me. I was taught that heaven and hell were "states of mind" and I was creating them by my thoughts. I was told that "God is love and does not hate. God is all there is. God is everywhere present; therefore, there is no place where God is *not*. Hence, God is all. *You* are here. God is *in* you; therefore, *you are good*. God is love, and hell is torture, and they cannot coexist unless we accept them as true—in which case, our subconscious minds will create them. Actual heaven and hell are simply scare tactics to keep the masses in line. You can't blame them for their elementary thinking; they don't know any better. But you're a Truth student, and you know the truth, etc."

And so any terrors that arose in my mind from hearing about judgment and hell and sin and repentance were quickly quelled by my self-reassurances (from my Unity books and other New Age material) that *I* was the one on the right higher, track and *they* were simply babes just learning to walk who didn't know any better. I'd go back to my *Metaphysical Bible Dictionary* and reassure myself that those born-again types didn't understand the deeper meanings of sin and repentance and so on. I actually pitied them.

This pity I felt at first wasn't from a sense of holier-than-thou arrogance or smugness of superiority. It was the same kind of thing a parent would feel when their six-year-old child begins pontificating on subjects such as parenting or life in general. You are amused, smile to yourself, and think, *Ah yes, I was once like that. But don't worry, little one. In time, you'll grow and learn and see the truth.*

I recall while in the third grade, a teacher suddenly brought up religion. She started asking the class questions such as where Adam and Eve came from and why God died on a cross. I was dumb-founded. "Why would God die on a cross?" That made *no* sense to someone who was raised believing that God is *not* a person but rather a "principle force." Furthermore, the New Age taught me that Adam and Eve and the garden of Eden were *allegorical, not literal.* I went home completely confused. I was relieved when my mother assured me that "those people aren't like us. They don't know the Truth as we do." It's funny because as a kid, you just assume *everybody* believes the same thing; and all of I sudden, I was hearing *very* different things.

It never occurred to me to ask my mother or Sunday school teachers *by what authority* they were insisting on their codebook being used to decipher the Bible. It never occurred to me that this *Metaphysical Bible Dictionary* and all the teachings of the New Age were dead wrong. It made me feel special to have the inside scoop on the mysteries of life.

I didn't understand that these teachers were being taught and, in turn, were teaching others (with great authority) some things about the Bible that were simply not true. They were all so pleasant, positive, loving, and completely sincere.

I realize today that distorting God's Word is how the devil oper-ates. From his first lie in the garden of Eden, "You will not surely die" (Gen. 3:4), right up to this present moment, his purpose is the same—dissuade anyone from taking God at his word. His goal is to cast as much doubt and deception as possible. The *last thing* the devil wants is for anyone to come to Jesus for the remission of sins.

The New Age deprives the world of the truth of the scriptures. It keeps man in the dark *while convincing him that he's in the light.* Imagine a grandparent writing a heartfelt letter to their grandchildren. They write it clearly and with intention. They give instruction; they say what they mean and mean what they say. Suppose they send the letter, but it's intercepted by an enemy (posing as a friend) who *purposely* misreads and distorts the letter to the trusting grandchild. They would say, "Well, here's what grandma *wrote*, but what she *meant* was this." The grandchild *faithfully accepts without question* whatever this reader says yet all the while receives an *entirely* different message than what was originally intended *to their utter detriment and demise.*

Some Christian churches have crosses on the walls or pulpit. Some have the outline of the Holy Spirit dove descending. In San Diego, I attended a Religious Science (Science of the Mind) church where they had the symbols of *every religion* on the wall. It reminded me of those "Coexist" bumper stickers where the letters are formed by the various religious symbols. The idea is that all religions have some truth in them, and we choose to draw the best from each. According to them, there isn't only one way to enlightenment (heaven). New Agers believe there are myriads of ways, and each must choose their own way according to this capacity at the time.

It wasn't until after my conversion and reading my Bible that I discovered the very simple verse where Jesus declares, "I am the way, the truth, and the life. No one comes to the Father except through Me" (John 14:6). And speaking of Jesus Christ, Peter specifically states in Acts 4:12, "Nor is there salvation in any other, for there is no other name under heaven given among men by which we must be saved." The New Ager will say that Christ represents the God-spark within us and that heaven is the state of mind of complete freedom and bliss. Therefore, when one accepts once and for all their true divine self, that divine self will then sprout and demonstrate that heavenly state of mind once and for all. They teach that this particular verse shows how the *only* way to experience this state of mind is to finally come after many lifetimes to the complete acceptance of our true nature. But if you read your Bible you'd never come to that conclusion at all.

If you have a system accepting all truths and another stating that it is the only and one truth, obviously they can't both be right! They may both be wrong or one wrong and the other right, but they can't both be right since the one *contradicts* the other.

I must emphasize again the life of joy a New Ager has. I certainly had a life of joy! Imagine waking every morning with the realization that your life is a self-fulfilling journey to happiness and completeness; that you were on your own path to an ever higher consciousness that only led to more joy and peace coming ultimately to cosmic consciousness; that *nothing* except your thoughts (which you control) could stand in your way; that you have an absolute assurance of this "truth" just as surely as a farmer who properly plants his crops does; and that when you "speak love to the universe, the universe responds and showers you with love."

I was taught how to include (at the end of my daily affirmations for whatever I wanted) the phrase "this or something better." This would assure me that if I did *not* get the thing I'd affirmed, then *certainly something* better was on its way. I'd turn it all over to the divine spark within me (which is my Christ) and get out of the way.

Naturally, I always had a spring in my step and brimmed with positivity. Who wouldn't? I'll tell you who—those folks who lived in negativity and weren't yet hip to the truth that their thoughts were, in fact, being planted into the subconscious minds which, in turn, churned out whatever was planted. We pitied those who weren't aware of their self-fulfilling negative experiences. It was a joy to tell them that they could, by their very thoughts and mental discipline, rise above these negative experiences and that if they'd just start expecting and acting as though their life would for good and positive things, it would inevitably be so. How could we be so sure? The law of cause and effect, that's how!

I'd begin each day with the daily devotional Unity publishes called the *Daily Word*. There was always a Bible verse accompanied by a New Age spin on that verse. I just assumed everything I read accurately taught from the Bible what the New Age said it taught. Because all New Age writings say the same thing, I was surrounded by reading material that always complimented and confirmed these beliefs.

I was also very quick to guard against negativity of any kind. For this reason, I always read my *Daily Word* the first thing in the morning. For years and years, I'd dutifully rise hours before the rest of the household to sit and read my metaphysical books, meditate, say and write my affirmations and denials, and look intently at my treasure map.

When you are convinced of this stuff, your positivity overflows into your life. I was a very positive person. Being positive also breeds confidence. People love to be around people with confidence. I was looked at as a leader because I always had that can-do attitude. Having a good attitude and pursuing excellence are good qualities, and they seemed to get me noticed. To me, the *only* things that stood between me and what I wanted were my thoughts and the time it took to "manifest" the things I desired.

Out of respect for certain individuals, I'm going to skip over years, details, and specific names of people who bore the brunt of my many mistakes, foolish decisions, and faulty belief system. I took several roads I thought were part of my rightful path. Unfortunately, those roads also involved people whom I had hurt and betrayed. I had made both major and minor life decisions solely on my ability to "rise above and overcome" any problems that might result in. If common sense said otherwise or people warned me of negative consequences, etc., I ignored them completely. (When you actually believe you're in the driver's seat, anyone who dares to "stomp on your dream" is known as a neggy—short for "negative person"—and becomes an enemy to your spiritual growth.) I truly believed I was literally in control. I thought I had the inside track. To demonstrate health, wealth, happiness, and peace, I only needed to plant those seeds. But of course, I was not in control. Stupid decisions result in avalanches of mistakes and missteps.

For instance, when I was twenty-two years old, I was assigned by the air force to a base in Tampa, Florida. I attended a New Age conference and was introduced to several "star children." You read that right. These people were convinced (and so was I) that they had migrated from several galaxies away to help us "find and develop the true light within us all." They spoke of the lament of the "galaxy elders" who regretted how Earth was one of the least developed planets in our solar system. One particular female star child explained the squalid conditions of our planet (and its inhabitants), including famine and wars, was due to the cause-effect manifestations of the "mass consciousness" of earthlings who were accepting and then creating this false reality. It was explained that as soon as earthlings looked within and fanned the inner spark of their higher self, things would dramatically improve. There was another speaker who particularly struck me. She said she had multiple visions and dreams that Tampa would be on fire as soon as Earth "awakened to its birth pangs," which would usher in a cosmic change, etc. She implied it would be best not to invest in anything or conduct major business transactions since *everything* was about to change forever. Now I was twenty-two and filled with positive ambition. Suddenly I was faced with a "what difference does it make, and what I do now?" mentality that put me into quite a slump. You see, my friends, when you do not have the truth, you have no anchor. Furthermore, when you embrace a *false truth*, you *think* you're anchored; yet all the while, you (in fact) believe a *lie*.

I turned to my Unity beliefs and was assured that no matter where I was "in consciousness," God was there too. The remedy was to continue on the road and trust my higher self who, after all, charted this entire path prior to my current incarnation.

But for all the positive thinking, I continued to make ill-advised and bad decisions that led to bad circumstances even though I was vehemently "affirming" otherwise.

I left the air force, moved to San Diego. I had others depending on me. I owed thousands in back taxes. I had creditors looking to repossess my vehicle. At the age of twenty-six, I had to declare a personal chapter 7 bankruptcy because I wasn't able to "affirm my way" out of debt. Do you have any idea how debilitating and humiliating all of this was? And who was to blame? Why, the person in the mirror I saw every day as I declared my personal affirmations! I was *not* demonstrating prosperity. It was my fault; the formula worked but I obviously wasn't "claiming my truth" sincerely enough. This is the only explanation a New Ager has. Things continued the downward spiral. I found myself shamefacedly going from "it works" to "what happened?" Of course, in the New Age, you already *know* what happened. I was "demonstrating" whatever my subconscious was being told to sprout, and I was the only one who could tell it what to sprout next!

I was also taught that *we attract* into our lives the *persons, places,* and *situations* designed to advance our growth and to learn those lessons we had set off to learn prior to our incarnation. We have our checklist items (developed *between lifetimes*) we seek to fulfill with each go-around. In truth, this is incredibly damaging because you can easily excuse yourself for harming. Take the person who's married who then decides they've "learned the lessons" necessary and see no further need to remain married. They move on, believing they're simply checking off their boxes. So they divorce, and there's great pain for the spouse. If there are children involved, it only gets worse. The hurt feelings and damage caused to others in the wake of this selfish mindset are ignored at least and justified at best. And of course, it helps to alleviate any guilt by *convincing yourself the spouses or children they're leaving are also drawing these experiences in order to learn those "valuable lessons" on their own checklists.* It becomes easy to assuage one's guilt from divorce, adultery, covetousness, selfish ambition, abortion, and so forth. After all, these things are all part of the great lessons as we move forward and attract those things into and out of our lives for our greater good.

How My Achilles' Heel Was Exposed

At the age of twenty-six, I left the air force and began a job in sales. I had my affirmations and goals and enjoyed moderate success. Then one day, I was introduced to a new salesperson and was asked to show him the ropes. I still remember the day we were standing on the beach. The girls in the bikinis were all around, and I made a crude comment.

He looked at me and said, "Hey, don't say that. Don't you know that it says in the Bible not to lust?"

Oh no! Not one of *those*! I said, "Don't tell me you're a born-again Christian."

He said he was.

I thought to myself, *Great! Here we go again*, and prepared to do battle using my "superior knowledge."

He was very nice, and I was cordial to him as I was to all the people I met. And why not? I was after all a "light-bearer" and a Truth student; thus, my positivity oozed out of me. We'd get into friendly discussions and arguments over the Bible, God, Jesus, etc. We'd go round and round. Between my two favorite weapons ("That's just *your* interpretation" and "You have to interpret these things metaphysically, etc."), I tried to hold my own. Convoluting things further was the fact that although we were using the same biblical words, they held different meanings to us both. For me, those words were defined by my trusty *Metaphysical Bible Dictionary*. For my friend, those words were defined by the Bible.

During one of our discussions, my friend asked, "Why did Jesus die?"

I was ready for this because over the years, my ministers and Sunday school teachers addressed that question. Without hesitation, I answered, "Because the Bible says the last enemy to be destroyed is death." Now this is true. It's a direct quote from 1 Corinthians 15:26.

You see, that verse *is* in the Bible, but it's used in the New Age in a completely different way. According to what I had been taught, Jesus was *just a man* who had been perfecting his own awareness of the "Christ consciousness" over many lifetimes. His particular reincarnation was to be his last because he had perfected his consciousness that he was able to "rise above" the constraints of death. He proved it by rising from the dead; that is, he had achieved full Christ consciousness and would no longer have to repeat the cycles of life, death, and reincarnation. (By the way, Unity denies the bodily resurrection of Jesus and declares that it was spiritual only.) He had finally hit the mark and came to show the world that it could be done. We learned that Jesus was just one of many "ascended masters" who had purified and perfected their Christ consciousness and thus had overcome the "last enemy," which was death. He and others would frequently visit the earth to show us the "higher truths." I realize how absurd this may seem to you who know the scriptures. But believe me, there are people reading this very page who see no problem with this explanation.

To my friend's great credit, our discussions were always friendly and frequent. Every time he'd raise an issue, I'd just deflect and say we had different interpretations. I'd go to my church and come back all fired up on Monday. He'd tell me about his church, and I'd smile but knew he wasn't quite getting it. We made a deal that I'd go to his church and he'd come to mine. I went to his first and brought the girl I had been living with. It was quite the scene. I wore a suit and tie, and everybody there was dressed in casual clothes. The music wasn't what I was expecting either. Then the preaching started. It was the old "Jesus died for your sins" story I'd heard for years. At the end, they gave an "invitation" to those who wanted to "accept Christ." I leaned over to my girlfriend and smugly whispered, "This is where they try to recruit you." I left that church service unimpressed and determined more and more that I was on the right track. I remember going to my church the following Sunday and during the service thinking, "My friend isn't going to like this at all, and we're only going to end up arguing again. And I'm really getting tired of his nagging." So I put off asking him to accompany me.

Then one day, out of the blue it happened. We were at the office having yet another "spiritual discussion" when my friend shot an arrow right through my Achilles' heel. I never saw it coming, and I wasn't prepared either. I had never been shaken like this before. It was sort of like a punch that lands and at first seems harmless. Then a few seconds later, you realize that serious damage has been done because you can feel it. My friend uttered three sentences that paralyzed me. (Of course, in hindsight I understand that the Lord himself was at the back of it all.)

Here's how it happened. My friend said, "Taylor, you were indoctrinated with what you believe. In other words, if you were on a desert island and read the Bible for yourself, you'd never have come to the conclusions you've come to about God and Jesus and life. Someone had to teach and tell you those things because they're *not* in the Bible."

Wow. Those were very reasonable statements! I actually felt my knees weaken. All I could think of was, *What if he's right?* For the first time, I was really stunned, shaken, and even a little scared. All my life, I had held to the principles that my mother and Unity had assured me were the truth. I was unwavering and unflappable (and extremely obnoxious). I began to realize that (other than the New Age spin) there are no verses that support one's freedom to hold a "metaphysical" interpretation. There are no verses that supported reincarnation. (Mind you, Unity has a few verses they'd cling to, but anyone reading those verses in context would never conclude that they were teaching reincarnation.)

There were no verses that actually say that "thoughts are things" or that man is "basically good" (quite the contrary, the Bible is not flattering to man at all!). There were no verses that taught that heaven and hell were states of mind or that Jesus was just a man who was working out the last go-around before ascending to the "higher con- sciousness." There were no verses that supported my *Metaphysical*

Bible Dictionary definitions. I need to state something else here lest someone reading this will think, *Well, why didn't you just* read *the Bible and find out?* The cofounder of Unity (Charles Fillmore) wrote, "Scripture may be a satisfactory authority for those who are not themselves in direct communion with the Lord" (*Twelve Powers of Man* 1930, 114). As one theologian puts it, "From this it is at once obvious that Scripture is for those dwelling on a lower plane of spiritual development, whereas personal experience with God transcends the authority of scripture!" Who wants to be known as the one who is "not yet in direct in communion with the Lord"? It was better to be the Truth student who relies on his teachers and masters to properly and metaphysically interpret the Bible in order to bring us the highest possible truth. This is the devil's version of FOMO (fear of missing out)! It's as though the devil whispers, "While you're busy reading your little Bible, others are in *direct* communion with their higher selves and are thus progressing much more nicely than you are."

Back to those three questions that shot through my Achilles' heel. I kept wondering, *What if he's right? If I'm honest, it's true. I really was taught all that stuff, but I've never actually read the Bible except for the texts from the entirety of their writings, which they then applied their particular spin upon. How could I possibly know the context?* These thoughts haunted me because I really did hold the Bible in high regard. I actually got to the point where I told myself, "Maybe I should say that sinner's prayer thing I've heard over the years heard just in case." I used to mock people who asked if I was "saved" by saying, "Saved from *what?*" And as soon as they launched into the hell thing, I'd dismiss it because I *knew* hell was only a state of mind.

It was not long after this that my world started crashing around me. I had already suffered some emotional and financial defeats due to the circumstances I was in. In my *misinformed arrogance* and *high-and-mighty "spirituality,"* I had also caused a lot of devastation and pain to a number of people. I had broken promises and lied, along with other behaviors, without the slightest regard for how it affected others. My affirmations (also called spiritual mind treatments in some New Age circles) kept coming up short. I was convinced that my subconscious was still producing leftover negative vibes from somewhere in the past (or even past lifetime). I was "doing the work," but *nothing* good was happening. By the way, the New Age is crafted very well by the devil because it keeps all the focus and blame on the individual. "It's not the *garden's* fault if there are weeds but the *gardener's*" was a statement that stung me over and again. It's also sinister in the opposite direction. Whenever you succeed in "demonstrations" and "manifestations" (i.e., whenever the things you've affirmed or denied come to pass in your favor), you're reinvigorated into perpetuating the lie.

In spite of my failures to "demonstrate," did I surrender to my friend? My pride wouldn't permit it! I was so desperate to plant new thoughts and *so* convinced that they'd "sprout" that for a while, I set a timer on my watch during the day so *every* hour of every day, it would beep and I'd stop what I was doing and spend five or so minutes in solid, concentrated meditations to pull me out of the swamp I found myself in. Panic was overwhelming me because I had *never* been in this kind of tailspin before. I had a Bible in my desk at work (which was presented to my mother from the teamsters at my father's funeral) and would turn to Psalms over and over again. Life felt like a weight crushing choking me. Now I'd had plenty of stressful times in the past, but this was *crushing* me.

And on top of these circumstances comes the arrow to my Achilles' heel! From that day forward (and for the *first time* in my life), I began questioning the New Age and trembling that I might, after all, be *wrong*. Understand, my entire belief system (which I had staked *every* life decision upon, whether major or minor, and would have been willing to die for) was suddenly kicked out from underneath me.

At the age of thirty-one and finding myself depressed, morose, and filled with bitter hopelessness—the likes of which I had *never* experienced—I went to the office of my friend. I didn't want him to see my panic or know my dire state (I was so proud). I tried to fake it and casually blurted out, "Okay then, one more time. What's the deal with this Jesus thing?"

He happened to be a home fellowship Bible teacher who, that evening, was teaching from Romans 5. Due to our most recent debate, he was understandably disgusted with me and thought I was mocking him again. (Mind you, we had been round and round for a year at this point.) He opened his Bible to the fifth chapter of Romans, placed it on the desk in front of me, and said, "I've had it with you. This is what I'm talking about tonight, and you can read it for yourself."

I picked up the Bible. As I slowly and tremblingly read the chapter, I could feel tears. The words were actually making sense now. Three times that chapter states how through one man (Adam), sin entered which, in turn, was passed on to *all his progeny*; yet through *another* Man (Jesus), *righteousness entered*, and *his righteousness was imputed to all* who believe in him. The point is stressed again in 1 Corinthians 15:21–22, "For since by man came death, by Man also came the resurrection of the dead. For as in Adam all die, even so in Christ all shall be made alive."

Naturally at that point, I did not understand anything about federal headship or propitiation or imputed righteousness or the Lamb of God or cleansing by the blood. But at that moment, right there in that office, a light dawned over me; and it was a biggie. I suddenly became aware that all the metaphysical spin I had learned couldn't hold a candle to what was becoming crystal clear right in front of my eyes. All of a sudden, I got it!

As somebody had once put it, I wasn't a sinner *because* I sinned. Rather, I sinned because I *was* a sinner. That's what those verses in the fifth chapter of Romans (and elsewhere) declared. And the sin *wasn't*, as the New Age taught me, in *believing* that I was separate from my God-spark! It was *disobeying* God which, in fact, actually separated me. The biblical definition of *sin* is "disobeying God himself" (1 John 3:4). This is clearly taught in scripture. Sin actually separates us from God.

> Behold, the Lord's hand is not shortened that it cannot save; nor His ear heavy that it cannot hear. But your iniquities have separated you from your God; ad your sins have hidden His face from you, so that He will not hear. (Isa. 59:1–2)

That's what Adam did. He flatly disobeyed God. According to the Bible, Adam is our federal representative. Romans 5:12 states, "Through one man sin entered the world, and death through sin, and thus death spread to all men, because all sinned."

The bloodline was polluted for every human being born ever since (Jesus is the exception since he was conceived by the Holy Spirit according to the Bible). There was the *original sin* (the sin Adam committed which, in turn, polluted every human born since), and then there was the *actual sin* (the sins of natural consequence that everyone who is born commits). And it was right there in black and white, in the pages of the Bible I was holding—the very book I held in high esteem. It was just me, the Bible, and God Almighty without the metaphysical interpretations to deceive me. I had never seen this before. I had never *really* understood it before. But there it was—despair and hope in one verse! I am doomed, but salvation is offered and secured to whoever comes to God on his terms of repentance and faith.

I was thunderstruck with the revelation that everything I had held dear—*everything* I had ever believed concerning all things spiritual, my life, my beliefs, and my most heartfelt and held convictions—was *utterly false*. I had been living and conducting my entire life based upon *lies*. All my life decisions, both minor and major, were made while holding onto beliefs that were not ever true. I don't speak Latin, but if I did, the best phrase to describe my life and all the things I held dear in Unity would be *crockus maximus*.

I now saw and understood that neither Unity nor New Thought or any of the tenets of the New Age *held any truth at all*. All false religions are based on distracting people from the *real* truth. It turns out the real truth is that Jesus Christ came to the earth to graciously *give his life as payment* for many so they would never have to face the wrath of God. Why is the price of payment Jesus's life? Because as Romans 6:23 puts it, "The wages of sin is death." When we who are owned by our Creator God disobey him, we bring death (*eternal death*) to ourselves. And we do this because we are born with a sin nature that can do nothing *but* sin. This truth is declared over and again in our Bible—Old Testament, New Testament, everywhere.

God Almighty in Ezekiel 18:4 declares, "Behold, all souls are Mine; the soul of the father as well as the soul of the son is Mine; the soul who sins shall die." So here in the single verse of Romans 6:23, we have the worst news we can ever and the best news we can ever hear, "The wages of sin is death but the free gift of God is eternal life in Christ Jesus our Lord."

I cannot adequately express the emotions of fear, joy, and relief that rushed upon me. There was something else. My eyes were opened. I got it! Later as I read my Bible, I felt I could relate to what it must have been like for Saul of Tarsus (Acts 9) to live all those years completely and utterly convinced that he was on the right track. Then out of the blue, God sovereignly opened his eyes to the truth, and this truth is not just about turning over a new leaf. It's becoming a new creation (2 Cor. 5:17). The truth is not just about what *is* true but also the certainty of what is *not* true. I thought of how I was as zealous and blind and enraged as Saul was. I was vehement about my false beliefs. Although unlike Saul, I did not seek to punish, torture, or imprison those who didn't agree with me (see Acts 9). However, like Saul (who later became Paul), *once I knew biblical the truth*, I was also provoked by all the false religious lies I saw all around me (see Acts 17).

I really and truly was a sinner according to the Bible's definition. I really and truly was thumbing my nose at God. And all this time, I was under condemnation.

Jesus *wasn't* some ascended master. He is God Almighty Incarnate. That's precisely what is succinctly stated in John 1:1, 14, "In the beginning was the Word, and the Word was with God, and the Word was God. And the Word became flesh and dwelt among us."

It all clicked. Jesus really was the Lamb of God who takes away the sin of the world. His work *actually* removes my sin and its penalty (John 1:29, 1 John 1:7). Furthermore, it was done *for* me because God is *gracious*. I learned that grace is an attitude in the mind of God whereby he, of his own free will and good pleasure, purposes to bestow eternal life upon the *unworthy, undeserving, ungodly*, and *rebellious* sinners. The lyrics to "Amazing Grace" thundered at me,

"Amazing grace, how sweet the sound, that saved a wretch like me. /
I once was lost but now am found, was blind but now I see."

I remember leaving my friend's office and going back to mine
in amazement. I sat at my desk trembling as I considered the facts.
Had I died any time before the moment I accepted the truth and cast
myself on the mercy of God, *I'd have been eternally in the very hell I
used to mock and deny*. It made me think of the millions of people
who go to their graves only to be immediately and consciously aware
of their eternal agony and torment and how there's *nothing* they can
do about it (Luke 16). Prior to that day, I had actually stood in front
of my friend and declared loudly with arms raised, "Okay, Satan, *if*
you're real and *if* you really exist, *enter me now!*" When nothing happened, I had mockingly said to my friend, "Do you see how stupid
your whole belief is?" And now I *knew* the truth! For the first time, I
trembled before God.

The first thing I did was attend my friend's church and the
home fellowship he taught. I was astonished and surprised at the
home fellowship as one by one, people I had never met before were
coming up to me and saying, "You're Taylor, right? We've been praying for you!" The following week, a woman from the home fellowship gave me a xeroxed chapter on Unity from Walter Martin's great
book *Kingdom of the Cults*. As I read his thorough analysis and biblical dismantling of Unity, I was again struck by the enormity of my
deception. I was also filled with joy and relief at having been rescued
from the lies and eternal damnation. That chapter was quite the eye-
opener as he further exposed things about Unity that I had never
known before.

It just so happened that my new church (this is the same one
my friend invited me to earlier) held a new believers class, which was
a six-week study of the Bible to introduce me more and more to the
Gospel, faith, and family of God. Within a week or so of my conversion, the church held a group baptism ceremony, and I couldn't wait!
I learned about baptism, what it was, and what it wasn't. I was so
excited to be baptized. It was held outdoors at one of the coves in San
Diego. There was a very large gathering of other new believers along
with friends and family. There were songs of praise, and the atmo-

sphere was electric for me. Long lines formed in front of each of the elders as we filed out into the water. One by one, I saw the baptisms. Then it was my turn. The fellow who baptized me asked if I wanted to say anything or pray. I stood there and prayed aloud to God and wept over how he saved me. I confessed how I had said, done, and believed so many things that were contrary to his Word and people. I was ashamed and astonished, and I was now fully forgiven. I was baptized. The peace and joy and love I experienced overwhelmed me. The words from 2 Corinthians 5:17 overcame me, "Therefore, if anyone is in Christ he is a new creation. Old things have passed away, behold all things have become new."

I had a new life, but I also had the reality of a long list of people I had hurt, offended, or destroyed in my "old life" of sin and rebellion. I met with (or called and wrote) as many as I could. I did my best to explain how I had been saved. I confessed and admitted to them the terrible things I had either done or said about them. I told them I did everything out of ignorance, pride, selfishness, and disregard for them. I apologized and asked for their forgiveness. To my great relief and joy, many of them did forgive me, and we were reconciled. I even found that many were already believers themselves! Sadly, some of whom I had injured didn't want to give me the time of day, and even as of this writing, we remain estranged. I don't blame them. I was a rat. I destroyed the lives of several people.

I began to attend church and read and study my Bible with fresh eyes and a new understanding. I became more and more aware of the deceitfulness of the New Age's teachings. Everything was so new, and the peace and joy I had were indescribable. I took communion for the first time and with an understanding of what it meant. I also came to realize I could no longer continue living with my girlfriend and made arrangements to move out as soon as possible. I remember our talk. I told her something had happened. I tried my best to explain how the things I'd thought were true (regarding my former beliefs) turned out to be lies and that the Bible alone held the truth. I said I wanted to be obedient to the Bible, and that meant we couldn't live together anymore. I remember at work the following day when another coworker asked me about my plans for the week-end. Without even thinking about it, I replied, "Well, I'm moving out from my girlfriend's place into one of my own." My coworker said he was sorry to hear we were breaking up. I explained (for the first time and somewhat awkwardly) that we hadn't broken up, that I was now a born-again Christian, and that it was something I wanted to do to honor God. I still remember the look on coworker's face.

But there was more. I experienced what other believers told me was my "honeymoon" with God. Several major circumstances changed dramatically and quickly for the better. I was learning to trust God more and more. I felt I was on top of the world! Now I'd sit and talk with my friend, but we weren't arguing anymore! Rather, I was filled with questions, and we'd marvel at God's grace in opening my eyes and rescuing me.

But then came one of the most painful emotional experiences I had ever felt in my life. It became clear that I could no longer be in a relationship with the woman I had been living with. Mind you, this woman wasn't just a girlfriend; I was convinced she was my soul mate. Prior to my conversion and in my great ignorance, I had done several horrible, bad, and sinful things in order to be with her. And I did those things because I was convinced we were destined. As it became more and more obvious that she and I wouldn't last, I panicked (which is stating it mildly). Immediately after my conversion, I was blessed in numerous ways; and now for the first time, *something was being removed from my life.* I had heard the word *codependent* before, but I never fully understood it until that moment. I had no idea how badly and emotionally I was attached. When you see a relationship begin to crumble and are convinced that "this one will last," it's heart-wrenching. I thought of all the things I had done in order to be with this person, and now it was going to be over.

One of the most valuable and early moments of my new life in Christ happened just as this soulmate relationship was beginning to fray. It was after a church service and I was speaking to my friend's sister-in-law who was also a believer. I didn't want to get into specifics with her, but I did let her know I felt like I was going through the wringer.

Very casually, warmly, and with great empathy, she said, "Oh, well, you're just going through a trial." It was sort of like a slow-acting lightning bolt.

I looked at her and asked, "Wait... I'm...in...a *trial*?"

She explained that although my soul was secure in Christ from here on, God himself was maturing me, conforming me into the image of Christ, purging things from my life and heart, etc., that were no longer edifying or of his will for me.

I looked at the various passages on trials such as Romans 5:3–4, James 1:2–5, and 2 Corinthians 12:7–10. As I dwelt on these passages, tears came to my eyes. Unlike Unity's god who was a mere *principle* and *life force*, I came to see even clearer that we have a personal God. I saw that God is intimately acquainted with me (Ps. 139) and was guiding *every single step* of my life for my good and his glory (Rom. 8:28). This was the God of the Bible, and as the psalmist declared, the Lord *really is* my shepherd. No matter what the issue of the trial is, the trials themselves are ordained by God for my good. This peace has stayed with me ever since. I can now say without fear of contradiction that I know two things for certain, and these two things apply to every believer. First, everything really is going to work out just fine. Second, the odds are pretty good that they're *not going to work out the way I think they should*. After all, God's ways are higher than our ways. He is infinite, and I am not. Moreover, God has all the knowledge and knows what he's doing; whereas I am fallen, finite, and have very limited knowledge. The relief this truth brings cannot be overstated. And best of all, it's a relief based upon the Holy Scriptures and not reliance on positive thinking.

I began discussing this with my friend who had been so instrumental in leading me to the Lord. He said something next that really got me. He told me to consider the possibility that I was *making an idol* out of this girl and our relationship. I remember I had attended a church service where the preacher said something like "You can always tell if you're making an idol out of something by the way you act when you don't get it." Despite knowing my sins were forever removed and forgiven, despite knowing peace as I had never known in my life, and despite being assured I was now living as an adopted member of the family of God, I felt myself panicking as this relationship dissolved. We had dreams of being together and getting married someday. I'd love to write here how maturely I handled it, but I can't. This was so devastating and emotionally crippling that I actually started questioning my new found faith and even considered that perhaps Unity was right after all. I hadn't come to grips with the great passage from Proverbs 3:5–8.

> Trust in the Lord with all your heart, and lean not on your own understanding; In all your ways acknowledge Him, and He shall direct your paths. Do not be wise in your own eyes; Fear the Lord and depart from evil. It will be health to your flesh, and strength to your bones.

But how can this end? I was going to marry this woman! was all I could think of. It became unbearable for me. My friend assured me over and over, saying, "God is still on the throne, and he knows what he's doing." Once my emotions settled down (which took longer than I care to admit), I recalled the old saying that it's better to "have Mrs. Right instead of Mrs. Right Now." In my foolish and stubborn mindedness, I purposely clung to this relationship even though the Lord had "closed the door" and did so in such a convincing way. And then the bottom fell out. The Lord closed the door for good. It was excruciating. To my friend's credit, he never said, "I told you so." But he was gracious and patient with me and helped me a lot.

While I was seemingly drowning in my (selfish) grief, my friend said something else that struck me, "Taylor, if this girl is the one for you, then God will make sure you'll stay together. *But what if there's a woman out there the Lord has chosen for you instead, someone who really loves the Lord and wants to be a godly wife but you haven't even met her yet?* What if God is maturing you and making you stop to focus solely on him and his will and his Word?"

I really wanted to believe that, and I accepted 100 percent that I had made an idol out of the relationship with the one I thought was my soul mate. I could see this clearly, although my heart still ached. I knew I had to walk away from this relationship. It felt like getting stabbed. I wanted badly to believe my friend. Soon enough, the pain went away as I busied myself in learning more and more about the Bible and the truth. Time passed, and then one day, before I knew it, *I met her*—the one my friend told me about (whom neither of us had even met yet). Perhaps one day, she'll write a book of her own; but suffice it to say, we've been blessed now with twenty-eight years of marriage and six wonderful children. It's better than anything I could have ever imagined or thought! I love to tell this story to others who are heartbroken over "the one who got away" and to encourage them to keep trusting God. I could never in a million years have predicted the joy, happiness, love, and comfort my marriage has brought me. When I compare it to what I was clinging to in my ignorance, I shake my head at my foolishness. Every day I thank God for my beautiful wife, marriage, and children.

I remember hearing a sermon about our trials and the reasons for them. I was constantly reminded of the grace of God. One of the pastors had a favorite saying that "God is just taking me on a journey." In hindsight, I was embarrassed at how little faith I had as God ended a relationship whilst bringing me my true love. Of course, God worked everything out. It is a wonderful truth that everything that happens in my life is for my good and God's glory (Rom. 8:28). It's a wonderful thing to understand that God not only loves me and has proven that love but is also actually involved in every single area and moment of my life.

In seeking to grow more and more in the grace and knowledge of God, I began reading and studying my Bible. Thankfully the church I attended offered wonderful midweek studies and discipleship classes.

Naturally, I had plenty of questions and was thankful that my friend made time to answer them. I found Walter Martin's great book *Kingdom of the Cults* extremely helpful because he not only articulated precisely what Unity taught but also soundly refuted even their most basic claims using Scripture. I highly recommend this book because he treats *all the other cults* the same way—a thorough review of what they believe and why they believe it is then followed by sound scriptural arguments disproving their system. Another extremely helpful resource for me was Josh McDowell's great work *Answers to Tough Questions Skeptics Ask About the Christian Faith.* This paperback book is packed with concise questions and answers along with recommendations for further studies, etc.

Not only did reading my Bible become pure joy, but I was also amazed at how many passages I had come across that Unity loved to quote, only to find out that they had taken all those verses *completely out of context* to mean something else entirely.

Remember that all-important question and statement from earlier? Of the sum total of your Christian knowledge, what percentage of it is owing to what somebody *told you* the Bible said versus what you've *actually read, in context,* for yourself? Your answer to that question will determine how susceptible you are to being deceived by cults and false religions, leading to a false worldview and eventually damnation.

Here are actual illustrations I was taught that shaped my beliefs while I was in the New Age. Now remember, these are biblical passages; therefore, I accepted them and their metaphysical explanations without question.

I recall hearing a recorded lecture by Ernest Holmes (Science of Mind) where he took a single verse and expounded the secrets to all health, wealth, and happiness. It was a (partial) quote from Proverbs 23:7, "For as he thinks in his heart, so is he." Now if you believed your thoughts controlled your life (and everything in it), you'd see this verse as the perfect "cause and effect" reason for everything! Why am I poor or sick or lonely or unhappy? Why, for the very same reason that others are prosperous, healthy, fulfilled, and happy! Because the Bible says (and we all agree the Bible is a pretty important book of instruction on life), "*As* a man thinks in his *heart*, so is he!" There's your answer! Start thinking properly because *as* you think in your *heart*, so will you be! Hallelujah!

That was all I needed! This is just one of the hundreds of examples of being led astray because somebody quoted a partial scripture out of context and assigned their own meaning to it since that meaning supports their existing mindset.

Here's the actual verse in context. I'm quoting from the New American Standard Version and the New King James version in order to give the fullest possible context. Here it is.

> Do not eat the bread of a selfish man, or desire his delicacies; For as he thinks within himself, so he is. He says to you, "Eat and drink!" But his heart is not with you. You will vomit up the morsel you have eaten, and waste your compliments. (Prov. 23:6–8 NASB)

> "Do not eat the bread of a miser, nor desire his delicacies; For as he thinks in his heart, so is he. "Eat and drink!" he says to you, but his heart is not with you. The morsel you have eaten, you will vomit up, and waste your pleasant words. (Prov. 23:6–8 NKJV)

Now honestly, dear reader, when you read these words, do you come away thinking that this text teaches that your thoughts control your life? Do these verses offer the secrets of attracting what you desire most? Of course, they don't. This verse warns of the dangers of dealing with hypocrites.

Furthermore, when Jesus rose from the dead, does the Bible teach (as the New Age claims) that Jesus did so in order to show all of us how, by fully fanning that God-spark into a blazing flame, one could overcome physical death? That one could thereby graduate beyond the necessity of numerous reincarnations and thus attain cosmic consciousness? The Bible teaches no such thing. Furthermore, Unity denies the bodily resurrection of Jesus (despite the fact that it is affirmed over and over in Scripture). The resurrection validates all that the Bible, God, and Jesus say about him. Let's face it. Anyone can *say* they'll rise from the dead in three days, but it's only the one who actually *does it* who validates that claim.

It's not just *that* Jesus died. It's *why* he died. It's also important to note that he was seen in public following his resurrection. It wasn't done in a closet.

But that's not what Unity and New Age would have you think. For years, I believed their teachings on the resurrection:

- "Jesus spent whole nights in prayer, according to the Gospels, and it is quite evident that He was resurrecting His body by realizing, as we do in our prayers, that God was His indwelling life" (Fillmore 1947, 13).
- "Eventually all souls reincarnate on earth as babes and in due time take up their problems where they left off at death" (*Teach Us to Pray*, 50).
- "We believe the dissolution of spirit, soul and body, caused by death, is annulled by rebirth of the same spirit and soul in another body here on earth. We believe the repeated reincarnations of man are the merciful provision of our loving Father to the end that all may come to obtain immortality through regeneration, as did Jesus" (*Unity Statement of Faith*, article 22).

Unity's views of the resurrection are confuted and refuted soundly by the Bible itself.

First Corinthians 15:3–6 says, "Christ died for our sins according to the Scriptures, and that He was buried, and that He rose again the third day according to the Scriptures, *and that He was seen by Cephas, then by the twelve. After that He was seen by over five hundred brethren at once* [italics added], of whom the greater part remain to the present, but some have fallen asleep."

Here are at least four things the Bible declares about the resurrection and what it proves (and no amount of *metaphysical spin* would lead anyone to believe otherwise):

1. *Jesus really is divine and the Son of God.* Romans 1:4 states that Christ was "declared to be the Son of God with power...by the resurrection from the dead." This equates

himself with God. The Jews certainly believed the equivocation. John 5:18 says, "The Jews sought all the more to kill Him because *He said that God was His Father, making Himself equal with God* [italics added]."

2. *The resurrection validates that the believer's sin was actually paid for.* First Corinthians 15:13, 17, 20 states, "But if there is no resurrection of the dead, then Christ is not risen. And if Christ is not risen, your faith is futile; you are still in your sins! But now Christ is risen from the dead." Ergo, since Christ *did* rise from the dead, your faith is *not futile*, nor are you in your sins any longer.

3. *The resurrection gives us a real and living hope of heaven no matter what happens to us here.* First Peter 1:3–5 says, "God, according to His abundant mercy has begotten us again to a *living hope through the resurrection of Jesus Christ from the dead* [italics added], to an inheritance incorruptible and undefiled and that does not fade away, reserved in heaven for you, who are kept by the power of God through faith for salvation ready to be revealed in the last time."

4. *The resurrection also assures us of a future judgment of the world.* Acts 17:30–31 states, "God commands all men everywhere to repent, because He has appointed a day on which He will judge the world in righteousness by the Man whom He has ordained. He has given assurance of this to all by raising Him from the dead."

There are no scriptures saying that Jesus's spiritual resurrection proved his mastery over never having to incarnate again. He did this in the place of sinners, and his death did what it was designed to do—deliver us forever.

> With His own blood He entered the Most Holy Place once for all, having obtained eternal redemption. (Heb. 9:12)

After I came to faith, I clearly saw how the New Age, rather than letting *Scripture interpret Scripture*, preferred to put their own slant and spin on the Holy Writ despite numerous warnings against that very thing.

It turns out Jesus didn't come to demonstrate his mastery over death so we could experience cosmic consciousness or nirvana. Matthew 20:28 and Mark 10:45 declare plainly (from Jesus's own lips) that he came to *give his life a ransom for many*. The New Age's reason for Jesus's coming to the earth and the Bible's reasons couldn't be more different! Jesus is declared by John the Baptist to be the Lamb of God who takes away the sin of the world, and the sin Jesus takes away isn't the "idea of a sense of separation from God." It's damnable sin that literally separates us from God and plunges us headlong into eternal misery. Scripture clearly states in John 3:18–19, "He who believes in Him [Jesus] is not condemned; but he who does not believe is condemned already, because he has not believed in the name of the only begotten Son of God." John 3:36 also says, "He who believes in the Son has everlasting life; and he who does not believe the Son shall not see life, but the wrath of God abides on him."

In the New Age, being born again is when you *come to the realization that you've been living a life completely ignorant of your true self and heritage*. You've been living a life of ignorance while carrying the divine spark and Christ's light within you. Here's a direct quote from Unity literature.

> Being "born-again" or 'born from above' is not a miraculous change that takes place in man; it is the establishment of that which has always existed as the perfect man idea of divine Mind. (*Christian Healing*, 24)

According to Unity, it's who you've always been; yet because you have not fully realized it, you've been living a perpetual self-fulfilling prophecy, unaware of the giant sleeping within. The New Age says that when you, like the prodigal son, come to your senses and realize the reality of what is truly yours, you'll "repent"—change your mind from dwelling on the negative shadows and accept who you really are. At that point, you'll begin your journey home. Lest you be discouraged on the way, they'll recite portions of the actual parable of the prodigal son (Luke 15:11–32) of how the son "came to himself"; that is, he realized that he was, in fact, divine and that the God-spark lived within him and how while the "son was yet a long way off, the father ran to him" to show you how the universe meets you more than halfway as you awaken to your true self.

By the same token, the New Age explains that when we begin our spiritual journey back to our rightful consciousness, we too will experience great things even if we only touched the outer edges (hem) of the "truth," only to be ever more realized as we progressed to possess not only the hem but also the entire garment.

These stories fascinated and excited me. They served to drive me harder and harder in my quest to have a more complete "realization of the presence of God" in order to grow and progress quicker and quicker through all the cosmic realms before me.

To the New Ager, heaven and hell are only states of mind (not actual realities). Since the "Christ" is that God-spark that is the *real* part of all of us, in order to experience a true heaven state of mind and its consequent demonstrations and manifestations (of pure health, happiness, prosperity, etc.), one must come to the realization that they are, in fact, bearing this divine spark that will then make itself real in the individual's life. I *actually* believed this. Thus, whenever one of those pesky born-again types asked, "Do you believe you need Christ in order to see heaven?" I'd answer, "I sure do!" and we'd shake hands and go our separate ways. We were using the same words, but the words held different definitions. His words held to the biblical definition; mine held to whatever my *Metaphysical Bible Dictionary* *told* me they meant. Consequently, we weren't even *close* to being on the same page!

I was well-intentioned and filled with all the positivity I could muster from believing the "truth." As the saying goes, "I was sincere but I was *sincerely wrong!*"

I remember another time in Unity when a minister was preaching on the need for forgiveness. Over and over, they'd say that unforgiveness only produces bitterness (which is true). They loved to quote a verse saying, "We must make it a priority to, as Jesus says, 'Loose them and let them go.'"

"Loose them and let them go"—that statement was tattooed in my mind. I knew that if I held bitterness, then karma would make sure I'd pay. I cannot tell you how many times I'd be angry with someone and would go into my meditations, picturing that person, determined to loose them and let them go. I would imagine that person as a young child in diapers and pitied them. I learned to love them; hence, with tears and a tremendous feeling of accomplishment, I'd say, "So-and-so, I'm no longer angry with you, and I hereby *loose you and let you go!*" I felt so great afterward. After all, that was in the Bible! Well, those words *are* in the Bible, but they have nothing to do with forgiving anyone. Those words are found in the Gospel of John. A man named Lazarus had died, and they were mourning his death. Jesus raised Lazarus from the grave. In John 11:43–44, we read, "Jesus cried with a loud voice, 'Lazarus, come forth!' And he who had died came out bound hand and foot with grave clothes, and his face was wrapped with a cloth. Jesus said to them, 'Loose him, and let him go.'"

"Loose him and let him go!" There it was! It's the only time those words are used in the Bible. Upon reading this, I couldn't help but chuckle in amusement and shake my head in shame. This was yet another example of their constantly misused, misquoted, or misapplied scriptures.

Jesus was right when he said, "You shall know the truth and the truth will set you free." Now the New Age taught that too, but their idea of truth and Jesus's meaning are completely different. For Jesus, the truth is found only in God's Word (our Bible).

> If you abide in *My word*, you are My disciples indeed. And you shall know the truth, and the truth shall make you free. (John 8:31–32; italics added)

In his prayer to the Father on behalf of his disciples and all believers, he prays, "Sanctify them by Your truth. Your word is truth" (John 17:17).

I sleep very well now. Because of Jesus's life and death, I've been rescued forever from God's wrath due to my sin. I've been rescued from the deceitful and twisted lies of the New Age and adopted into the kingdom and family of God. The Holy Spirit assures that I am growing in the grace and knowledge of the Lord.

I thank the Lord daily for having delivered me. When I see and compare the lives of my six children to what I was doing at their various ages, I again tremble and thank the Almighty God for calling me out of the darkness.

I've come to see now that there are basically four types of people:

1. There are those who are saved and know they're saved because they've obeyed God's command of "repentance toward God and faith toward our Lord Jesus Christ" (Acts 20:21).

2. There are those who are damned and know it, and they don't seem to care.

3. There are those who *think* they are saved but are, in fact, damned. They reject God's terms and seek to approach God *on their own terms*; that is, they rely on a false belief system. Paul describes them (as he did Israel in Romans 10) that "they have a zeal for God, but not according to knowledge. For they being ignorant of God's righteousness, *and seeking to establish their own righteousness, have not* [italics added] submitted to the righteousness of God." When those zealous and truly well-meaning folks come knocking on my door, I do my best to engage them. I explain to them that I too once thought I was on the right track. I tell them they've been indoctrinated, etc. I even ask them whether it bothers them at all that the books pertaining to their religion are in the cult section of any Christian bookstore!

4. There are those who *are* saved yet lack solid assurance—the assurance that comes as they grow in the grace and knowl-

edge of the Lord Jesus Christ and the scriptures. Somebody once said, "To have an assurance of your salvation is the *best* thing, but to doubt your salvation is the *next best* thing" because it drives you to examine yourself to make your calling and election sure.

People in the New Age speak a different language because they have a different understanding of what words mean. But don't stop praying for them. *Give* them this booklet in the hopes that they'll come to a saving knowledge of the truth. After all, if not by the grace of God, we who are now saved were also blind, lost, and on our way to eternal ruin.

Let's face it. If there's only *one* way to heaven (and according to the Bible, there is) then *every other way must be false*. Since the afterlife is forever, it behooves one to know what they know and why they know it. The clincher for me is the bodily resurrection of Jesus Christ. The resurrection *validates* that Jesus is precisely who he, the Father, and the scriptures declare he is. It validates that everything Jesus said is *true*.

One of the basic tenets of the New Age is that man is "basically good" since man is literally a divine beam and spark of the one God consciousness. If that were so, you'd think man would portray himself in a better light than what the Bible does. Clearly, the experience of everyday real life proves that man is nowhere *near* good and that iniquity abounds. The universal prevalence of lawlessness, injustice, murder, and cruelty can't be chalked up to a few rogue, bad eggs. *Does the Bible support the basic goodness and divine spark of each person?* Let's see.

The New Age tells us to "listen to your heart." If we were basically good, that would be excellent advice. But we are not. Let's see what the Bible says about our hearts and our goodness:

- "The heart is deceitful above all things, and desperately wicked, who can know it?" (Jer. 17:9).
- "There is none righteous, no, not one; There is none who understands; There is none who seeks after God. They have

75

all turned aside; they have together become unprofitable; There is none who does good, no, not one" (Rom. 3:10–12). I know many who say *they're searching* and seeking God. In truth, they're *not* seeking the God of the Bible but *only the benefits of health, wealth, and happiness.*

- "For there is not a just man on earth who does good and does not sin" (Eccles. 7:20).

- "Then the Lord saw that the wickedness of man was great in the earth, and that every intent of the thoughts of his heart was only evil continually" (Gen. 6:5).

- "But we are all like an unclean thing, and all our righteousnesses are like filthy rags; We all fade as a leaf, and our iniquities, like the wind, have taken us away. And there is no one who calls on Your name, who stirs himself up to take hold of You; for You have hidden Your face from us, and have consumed us because of our iniquities." (Isa. 64:6–7).

- "[Jesus is speaking,] 'For from within, *out of the heart of men*, proceed evil thoughts, adulteries, fornications, murders, thefts, covetousness, wickedness, deceit, lewdness, an evil eye, blasphemy, pride, foolishness. All these evil things come from within and defile a man'" (Mark 7:21–23; italics added).

The Bible soundly refutes every tenet of the New Age.

Reincarnation and resurrection are *mutually exclusive terms.* The former continues to be born over and again in various forms, races, genders, etc., in an attempt to purge away their shortcomings (sins!) to eventually reach the cosmic consciousness state.

Conversely, the resurrection is *once* and with the same (albeit glorified) body. When Jesus rose from the dead, there was no mistaking who he was. He spoke and ate in their presence. The New Age teaches reincarnation as a way for man to work through and be purged of his sins. The Bible does not. The Bible teaches that we die once, and then comes the judgment (Heb. 9:27). It teaches that

76

Jesus's sacrifice provided the once-for-all cleansing for our sins (Heb. 9:12).

Concerning our life purpose, the New Age declares the great do-it-yourself project of *attracting* health, wealth, and prosperity along with the ultimate goal of attaining cosmic consciousness.

Contrast this with the biblical call for repentance toward God and faith toward Jesus Christ. Why? Our disobedience toward God damns us, and we are born dead in trespasses and sins.

> God commands all men everywhere to repent, because He has appointed a day on which He will judge the world in righteousness by the Man whom He has ordained. He has given assurance of this to all by raising Him from the dead. (Acts 17:30–31)

> Unless you repent you will all likewise perish. (Luke 13:3–4)

> Most assuredly, I say to you, unless one is born again, he cannot see the kingdom of God. (John 3:3)

The New Age emphasizes do-it-yourself self-righteousness. The Bible teaches we must be absolutely perfect and righteous in order to see heaven and avoid hell. The Bible declares that the very righteousness we require is *provided* to us by Jesus Christ. This is a gracious act because it is given in spite of our sinfulness. The Bible declares that apart from grace, we have no hope.

A life devoted to our so-called higher self ignores the reality of sin and wrath that abides on every soul:

- "For what profit is it to a man if he gains the whole world, and loses his own soul? Or what will a man give in exchange for his soul?" (Matt. 16:26).

- "And do not fear those who kill the body but cannot kill the soul. But rather fear Him who is able to destroy both soul and body in hell" (Matt. 10:28).
- "And being in torments in hell, he lifted up his eyes and saw Abraham afar off, and Lazarus in his bosom" (Luke 16:23).
- "I have five brothers that he may testify to them, lest they also come to this place of torment" (Luke 16:28–29).
- "And anyone not found written in the Book of Life was cast into the lake of fire"(Rev. 20:15).
- "Now I urge you, brethren, note those who cause divisions and offenses, contrary to the doctrine which you learned, and avoid them. For those who are such do not serve our Lord Jesus Christ, but their own belly, and by smooth words and flattering speech deceive the hearts of the simple" (Rom. 16:17–18).
- "I marvel that you are turning away so soon from Him who called you in the grace of Christ, to a different gospel, which is not another; but there are some who trouble you and want to pervert the gospel of Christ. But even if we, or an angel from heaven, preach any other gospel to you than what we have preached to you, let him be accursed" (Gal. 1:6–8). *All* cults teach a "different gospel" that say they all seek a "works, self-righteousness approach." Religion tries to reach up to God, whereas the scriptures declare that *nobody* does that; rather, it is God himself who reaches down and saves sinful men.
- "You who love the Lord, hate evil! He *preserves the souls* of His saints" (Ps. 97:10; italics added).
- "Contend earnestly for *the faith* which was once for all delivered to the saints. For certain men have crept in unnoticed who long ago were marked out for this condemnation, ungodly men, who turn the grace of our God into lewdness and deny the only Lord God and our Lord Jesus Christ" (Jude 3–4; italics added).

The truth matters. Dear reader, by the time you finish this sentence, hundreds if not thousands of souls around the world will have passed away, some into everlasting life and the rest into eternal darkness, torment, and despair. There is nothing more important than the salvation of your eternal soul.

Additional Problems with the New Age

For a group who believes the Bible is their "basic textbook," they are unaware that the "name it and claim it" mindset begets covetousness and is in direct violation of the tenth commandment. God would never command we disobey him. This alone should warn anyone who thinks they're seeking the "truth" into seeing they're being manipulated by the very being they deny—the devil. It's not for nothing that Scripture declares in 1 John 2:15–17:

> Do not love the world or the things in the world. If anyone loves the world, the love of the Father is not in him. For all that is in the world—the lust of the flesh [pleasure], the lust of the eyes [possessions], and the pride of life [position, status]—is *not* [italics added] of the Father but is of the world. And the world is passing away, and the lust of it; but he who does the will of God abides forever.

First John 5:19 states, "The whole world lies under the sway of the wicked one." The devil, like God, is a real personal being.

The New Age teaches against the existence of a literal hell and punishment. It believes that everyone who dies is better off and will reincarnate to learn more and more lessons. The Bible clearly speaks of literal heaven and a literal hell, both of which are eternal. We are either eternally saved from God's wrath, or we shall endure it forever.

The New Age teaches that there are many roads to spiritual growth and heaven and enlightenment. The Bible declares there is only *one* God and only *one* way *to* God, and that way is Jesus Christ alone (John 14:6). Despite the New Age holding to the Bible as a basic textbook (to be considered along with additional writings), the Bible itself is declared to be the *sole authority for all matters of faith and practice*.

Paul wrote to Timothy (in 2 Timothy 3:16) that all Scripture is given by inspiration of God (literally "God-breathed"). More importantly, he admonished him thus in 2 Timothy 3:14–15.

> But you must continue in the things which you have learned and been assured of, knowing from whom you have learned them, and that from childhood you have *known the Holy Scriptures, which are able to make you wise for salvation through faith which is in Christ Jesus* [italics added].

All beliefs taught by the New Age along with all false religions are on a collision course with what the Bible says. *They can't both be true*. Many choose to change the Bible's clear teaching and intent *to fit their own belief systems* and believe they do so with impunity. The Bible itself emphatically begs to differ:

- "No prophecy of Scripture is of any private interpretation, for prophecy never came by the will of man, but holy men of God spoke as they were moved by the Holy Spirit" (2 Pet. 1:20–21).
- "All Scripture is given by inspiration of God, and is profitable for doctrine, for reproof, for correction, for instruction in righteousness, that the man of God may be complete, thoroughly equipped for every good work" (2 Tim. 3:16–17).
- "Every word of God is pure; He is a shield to those who put their trust in Him. Do not add to His words, lest He rebuke you, and you be found a liar" (Prov. 30:5–6).

- "For I testify to everyone who hears the words of the prophecy of this book: If anyone adds to these things, God will add to him the plagues that are written in this book; and if anyone takes away from the words of the book of this prophecy, God shall take away his part from the Book of Life, from the holy city, and from the things which are written in this book" (Rev. 22:18–19).

These verses clearly state that (1) *none* of the Bible is open to any private interpretation, (2) *all* Scripture is literally God-breathed and inspired, and (3) whoever changes anything in the Holy Scripture (whether *adding to, taking from,* or *misrepresenting*) shall be rebuked by the Almighty God himself. Yet that is *precisely* what all false religions, including New Age cults, do.

This is why the best question you can ask the false Christian cults who knock on your door is the same question from the beginning of this book: Of the sum total of your Christian knowledge, what percentage of it is owing to what somebody *told you* the Bible said versus what you've *actually read, in context,* for yourself?

This question hits home. I use it all the time. They'll always reply with something like "We do believe the Bible *but only insofar as its interpreted by our own scriptures.*" Then I challenge them with the same challenge that woke me up, "You were indoctrinated with what you believe. In other words, if you were on a desert island and read the Bible for yourself, you'd never have come to the conclusions you've come to about God and Jesus and life. Someone had to teach and tell you those things because they're *not* in the Bible." Jesus cannot be God *and* a created being. He cannot be Creator and created. Those categories are mutually exclusive. Furthermore, the Bible warns over and again against the false prophets by which many are led astray.

Some of the best people I know are devout, yet being sincere doesn't get you into heaven. I try my best to explain to them that I too was in a cult and thought I knew better, and I try to do so in a very uncondescending way. I'm not looking to embarrass them or come across as holier-than-thou. I'll quote them from Romans

10:2–4 with the same concern Paul had for his fellow Jews when he wrote:

> They have a zeal for God, but not according to knowledge. For they being ignorant of God's righteousness, and seeking to establish their own righteousness, have not submitted to the righteousness of God. For Christ is the end of the law for righteousness to everyone who believes.

There it is—a zeal for God! Boy, I sure had that just as all false religions do. They are fervent and sincere and disciplined. But that doesn't alter the fact that their beliefs are misplaced. That verse—"For they being ignorant of God's righteousness, and seeking to establish their own righteousness, have not submitted to the righteousness of God"—clearly shows that those sincere folks who seek to establish their "self-righteousness" have *not* submitted to God's way. If a person could get into heaven by their own efforts as Paul said in Galatians 2:21, then Christ died for nothing.

Some hear, and others will remain unconvinced.

Many people live as though John 3:16 says, "For God so loved the world that he gave Moses the Ten Commandments that whosoever *does their best or is sincere or practices the Golden Rule* or strictly adheres to the teachings of their particular founder, etc. will not perish but have everlasting life."

But the verse doesn't say that. All Scripture points to Christ alone as the only way to the Father. No one is exempt; we either come to God on his terms or we don't come at all. Listen to how the apostle Paul put it when defending salvation *by faith alone in Christ alone* in his letter to the Galatians.

> Knowing that a man is not justified by the works of the law but by faith in Jesus Christ, even we [the apostles!] have believed in Christ Jesus, that we might be justified by faith in Christ and not

by the works of the law; for by the works of the
law no flesh shall be justified. (Gal. 2:16)

Despite Unity and all the New Age's best efforts to say otherwise, the Bible can be summed up in one word—*redemption*. Jesus
Christ is the Redeemer, and whoever comes to him on his terms are
the redeemed.

The Bible could be broken down into three distinct sections
under redemption:

- From Genesis until Malachi, the heading is "Messiah
Is Coming." The Bible tells us that the Messiah would
come specifically to *bear our iniquities* (Isa. 53:11). It is
our actual iniquities that separate us from God and leave
us condemned (Isa. 59:1–2)—yet Christ made a full payment and satisfaction for something he did not do. He was
the innocent and perfect one who suffered *on behalf* of us,
sinners.
- The heading from the four Gospels along with the first
chapter of Acts would be "Messiah Is Here" (John 4:24–
26). Jesus was actually born in time and space and performed all that the Old Testament revealed the Messiah
would do.
- From the rest of Acts to Revelation, the heading would be
"Messiah Is Coming Again" (Titus 2:13).

The Bible also has fulfilled prophecies that are so incredibly
detailed that many critics have charged the writing of certain events
after the fact.

The New Age refuses to accept that while we are to *name and
claim the good we so richly deserve*, we are *literally storing up wrath and
judgment against ourselves* because of our refusal to come to God and
be reconciled on his terms.

But in accordance with your hardness and your
impenitent heart you are treasuring up for your-

self wrath in the day of wrath and revelation of
the righteous judgment of God, who "will render
to each one according to his deeds": eternal life
to those who by patient continuance in doing
good seek for glory, honor, and immortality; but
to those who are self-seeking and do not obey the
truth, but obey unrighteousness—indignation
and wrath, tribulation and anguish, on every soul
of man who does evil, of the Jew first and also of
the Greek; but glory, honor, and peace to everyone who works what is good, to the Jew first and
also to the Greek. For there is no partiality with
God. (Rom. 2:5–11)

Everything in the Bible from the garden of Eden to the
Incarnation and Crucifixion, the words of Jesus, historical narratives,
the parables, and even the conversion of Saul of Tarsus are seen and
taught differently in the New Age. Why? Because they are viewed
with their metaphysical spectacles, and they believe they are the
enlightened ones.

You see, when you are allowed (without challenge) to allegorize,
spiritualize, or reinterpret passages, you can make a convincing argument to the one who is blind.

Take the garden of Eden. According to the Bible, the garden of
Eden is a real geographical place. Adam and Eve were real flesh-and-
blood creations.

But when the New Age gets done with it, they have a very inter-
esting take. This is how it was explained to me by Unity ministers;
and it's all tied into naming and claiming, manifesting, and demonstrating *the good you so richly deserve*. According to the New Age,
Adam or man represents *intellect*. Eve or woman represents *emotions*.
When these two come together, the resultant offspring is the desired
demonstration. The desired outcome requires both, and when both
are applied, the outcome is certain unless you're doing it incorrectly
(always a convenient out when things aren't happening the way you
want). It's never the fault of the false system but rather the operator.

For example, in order to "demonstrate" your own reality, one must not only intellectually visualize the desired outcome but also create the feelings that would accompany such a demonstration. For example, you want to be a millionaire, so you find pictures in magazines or online that show the lavish life of such a person. You deliberately spend time gazing upon these images (because you're planting the seed!). You affirm that you are, in fact, a millionaire. But that's only the first part. Next, you must ask, "How would I *feel* if I were a millionaire?" So you intentionally begin to manufacture the feelings that could accompany this. In New Age term, this is *to act as though it's already so.*

This is the lie. The "compass" misled me over and over. Not only did I assiduously study, but I also was a youth leader in Unity in hopes of educating the young people about the wonderful realities of the New Age. The Lord only knows how many souls I had poisoned.

A Word About Manifestations, Demonstrations, and Miracles

Now I want to say something here that is important to understand, and that is *supernatural activities and events* do *actually happen.* I've read of numerous supernatural events that have taken place in people's lives. Whether it's a miracle, demonstrations of wealth and health, out-of-body experiences, near-death experiences where one sees the "light," etc. My own mother said she actually "saw" via astral projection my father's funeral three years before it happened.

I've seen those who've communicated with the spirit realm (beyond the hoax séances) with the Ouija board that had proof behind it (i.e., events predicted actually happened, etc.).

My mother had us all convinced that she was speaking with the other side and that she was, in fact, in regular contact with my deceased father.

I would never attempt to convince those who claim these experiences that these things didn't happen or weren't real. Who am I to say a person did or didn't have an experience?

I hear it all the time when speaking with New Agers, "But, Taylor, I have known people who had near-death experiences who don't report anything like what you're saying about the afterlife. They were assured there was no hell, etc." "But, Taylor, I've actually sat with psychics who've told me things that have come to pass." "But,

Taylor, I've actually seen my circumstances of health or wealth or happiness improved due to my positive affirmations."

We cannot deny what people experience. What can we conclude, then? We conclude they either imagined it or that it happened.

The Bible itself speaks of sorceries and magicians and charms. Here's the million-dollar question: Do we base our reality upon *our experience* or *upon the Word of God?* If you answered that you base your reality on what you (or others) supernaturally experience, then you will be misled.

"How can you say something like that with such arrogant certainty?" someone might ask. Like everything else, my response is based on the Bible, not what somebody *told* me.

To begin with, there is an invisible spiritual realm, and there are angels and demons. Demons can manipulate. We already know the devil knows the Bible, yet he is called the Great Deceiver.

Jesus put it plainly.

> It is written, "Man shall not live by bread alone,
> but by every word that proceeds from the mouth
> of God." (Matt. 4:4)

The Word of God *must* trump all else, including premonitions, experiences, etc., because the devil is in the deception business. Look at 2 Corinthians 11:13–15.

> For such are false apostles, deceitful workers, transforming themselves into apostles of Christ. And no wonder! For Satan himself transforms himself into an angel of light. Therefore it is no great thing if his ministers also transform themselves into ministers of righteousness, whose end will be according to their works.

When Moses and Aaron first approached pharaoh and cast his staff down, it became a serpent (Exod. 7:10). The next thing we read is that the pharaoh's magicians did likewise. God permits things to happen (otherwise they couldn't happen), but that does not mean he approves all things. We do not deny that these things take place. I personally enjoyed various times of "rising above situations" and experienced my own *demonstrations of sorts*. I've heard lots of people testify to their own experiences. This bolstered my faith and belief that I was on the right track. After all, there really *is* a spiritual realm! Someone or something is certainly moving that plastic indicator on the Ouija board! The Bible certainly doesn't dispute supernatural activity. The Bible warns against seeking mediums and wizards, inquiring after the dead, etc. This is because man, due to his fallen nature, is easily *misled* and *manipulated*. There really are demons who can testify to things and *manipulate* us. The Bible readily acknowledges this.

The question now becomes this: *Is our ultimate authority* our experience *or* the Word of God?

This is a good question because we're all looking for the truth.

According to the Bible, all things are to be measured against, validated, or disproved not by experience but by the Holy Scriptures, which are *inerrant* and *infallible*.

Certainly, supernatural occurrences actually happen. This we cannot deny. Even in Scripture, we see these occurrences. However, God expects us to use discernment in these things.

And what is to be our final authority for their authentication, whether they are of the Lord or demons? The scriptures! In addressing séances, contacting the dead, and mystical experiences, Isaiah 8:19–20 says:

> And when they say to you, "Seek those who are mediums and wizards, who whisper and mutter," should not a people seek their God? Should they seek the dead on behalf of the living? To the law and to the testimony! *If they do not speak according to this word, it is because there is no light in them* [italics added]."

There you have it.

Any experience or prophet (or minister or teacher) who corrupts or plainly teaches against the Holy Scriptures has "no light in them."

God *has* spoken, and he has done so with *finality* in his Word, the Bible.

Scripture provides us with the awareness of these phenomena along with serious warnings. Take the warning in Deuteronomy 13:1–5.

> If there arises among you a prophet or a dreamer of dreams, and he gives you a sign or a wonder, *and the sign or the wonder comes to pass, of which he spoke to you* [italics added], saying, "Let us go after other gods"—which you have not known— "and let us serve them," *you shall not listen* [italics added] to the words of that prophet or that dreamer of dreams, *for the Lord your God is testing you* [italics added] to know whether you love the Lord your God with all your heart and with all your soul. You shall walk after the Lord your God and fear Him, and keep His commandments and obey His voice; you shall serve Him and hold fast to Him. But that prophet or that dreamer of dreams shall be put to death, because he has spoken in order to turn you away from the Lord your God, who brought you out of the land of Egypt and redeemed you from the house of bondage, to entice you from the way in which the Lord your God commanded you to walk. So you shall put away the evil from your midst.

Here, we're clearly warned that even if a supernatural event takes place to authenticate the persons' powers, the moment they try to persuade you against the God of the Bible, they are not to be listened to. (In fact, God himself called for the capital punishment of such a deceiver.)

I'm amazed at how all the false teachers of today don't take this warning more to heart. Again, the penalty for being a false prophet in the Old Testament was *capital punishment.* Scripture also tells how to spot a false prophet. Simply stated, if they say something will happen and it doesn't happen, they're false prophets! (So much for these psychic hotlines that "guarantee" a higher probability rate than their competitors! According to the Bible, it had better be a 100 percent success rate 100 percent of the time, or they're to be dismissed as false.)

> The prophet *who presumes to speak* a word in My name, *which I have not commanded him to speak,* or who speaks in the name of other gods, that prophet shall die. And if you say in your heart, "How shall we know the word which the Lord has not spoken?"—when a prophet speaks in the name of the Lord, if the *thing does not happen or come to pass,* that is the thing which the Lord has not spoken; the prophet has spoken it presumptuously; you shall not be afraid of him. (Deut. 18:20–22; italics added)

In the first case, if a sign or wonder *does* come to pass and the person who performed it uses them as an opportunity to persuade you away from the God (and by extension his teachings) of the Bible, he is to be ignored. He is *false.*

Furthermore, when anyone speaks with authority "in the name of the Lord" and the thing he predicts *does not* come to pass as predicted, he too is to be ignored.

Our test for all matters of faith and practice is the Scripture. Any and all dreams, visions, people, experiences, or metaphysical interpretations that are contradicted by the Holy Scriptures are to be shunned and ignored.

This is God's loving concern over his sheep so they will not be misled.

These verses teach that any person who predicts and/or performs supernatural phenomena (to prove their authenticity) and then *uses that experience to lure you away* from the one true God is actually *seeking your destruction.*

Remember Paul's warning to the Galatians 1:8, "But even if we, or an angel from heaven, preach any other gospel to you than what we have preached to you, let him be accursed." Paul is saying even if an *apostle* or *angelic being* appears and preach "another" gospel, they are to be accursed. There is only *one* true Gospel. Jesus Christ came to save sinners from the wrath of God. His saving work is accomplished *for* us and given to us graciously without regard to *any* so-called merit (since we have none). That is the truth, and anything *else* is a lie and an abomination. Jesus himself warned us to expect very specific deceptions when he said in Matthew 24:24–25, "For false christs and false prophets will rise and show great signs and wonders to deceive, if possible, even the elect. See, I have told you beforehand." Signs and wonders may fill us with awe. They may cause us to accept and believe their authenticity, yet they are designed to mislead and deceive.

All false religions seek to misquote, misapply, or misinterpret Scripture. Martin Luther once said, "Every man must be able to read and interpret the Bible for himself, but he is not allowed to *misinterpret* the Bible for himself!" The Bible says what it means and means what it says.

When Scripture tells us to test all things to prove all things (1 Thess. 5:21, Rom. 12:2), it is so we may *know* what the Bible actually says in order to be certain. Popular sayings such as "God helps those who help themselves" or "Cleanliness is next to godliness" are not in the Bible.

There was once a woman who strenuously objected about her church having to go into debt in order to buy their own building. She stood before the church board and declared with authority, waving her Bible, "Be neither a borrower nor a lender! Be neither a borrower nor a lender!" She was quoting *Hamlet.*

The truth does make you free. But first you have to *know* it, and the only source of truth is the Holy Bible (2 Tim. 3:16, 2 Pet. 1:20–21, Prov. 30:5–6).

What Difference Does It Make?

When it comes to math, facts matter. When it comes to the *eternal destiny of your soul, truth* matters.

Contrast it to the New Age belief that teaches the power of attraction of health, wealth, and prosperity (which is unbiblical because it fosters covetousness) and the reality of possessing eternal life for any who come to God on his terms. The New Age denies eternal punishment and condemnation against the words found in the very Bible they claim to hold in high regard.

> He who believes in Him is not condemned; but he who does not believe is condemned already, because he has not believed in the name of the only begotten Son of God.
> He who believes in the Son has everlasting life; and he who does not believe the Son shall not see life, but the wrath of God abides on him. (John 3:18–19, 36)

> Most assuredly, I say to you, he who hears My word and believes in Him who sent Me has everlasting life, and shall not come into judgment, but has passed from death into life. (John 5:24)

The Bible declares that God *is* love (1 John 4:16); however, he is also just and must punish all iniquity. As a judge, he does punish it fully. The question for us is whether *we* will be punished ourselves

93

(as in the case of the self-righteous and unrepentant) or *will we repent and accept Jesus's punishment in our place*, purely of mercy and grace.

Our problem is not healing our "sense of separation" from God. The problem is we *are* separated from God; and as Jesus says, unless one is born again, he *cannot* see the kingdom of God.

Furthermore, the Bible declares there is only *one* God—the God of Abraham, Isaac, and Jacob. This is not my interpretation. This is what it actually declares. New Agers speak of "the Universe, a Higher Power, God or *whatever you choose to call it.*" This sounds as though nobody really knows for sure, so they want to cover their bases and remain open and inoffensive to others.

The Bible takes a completely different view:

- "I am the Lord, and there is no other; I form the light and create darkness, I make peace and create calamity; I, the Lord, do all these things" (Isa. 45:6-7).
- "Therefore know this day, and consider it in your heart, that the Lord Himself is God in heaven above and on the earth beneath; there is no other" (Deut. 4:38–39).
- Jesus declares in John 14:6, "I am the way, the truth, and the life. No one comes to the Father except through Me." This is an exclusive claim, and he wasn't talking about a "self-realization of the divine spark within." To come through Jesus is to accept that his death (and that alone) is what reconciled us to God. There is only one God and only one way *to* God. According to the Bible, those who either ignore or refuse this do so at their great peril.
- When we get right down to it, we are either believers or unbelievers, saved or unsaved, and redeemed or condemned based solely on whether or not we repent and accept the Lord's provision for our sin, which he willingly provided on the cross in his death. First Corinthians 1:18 makes it clear, "The message of the cross is foolishness to those who are perishing, but to us who are being saved it is the power of God."

This salvation is precisely why Jesus came. When the apostle John penned the Gospel of John, he concluded it with these words from John 20:30–31.

> And truly Jesus did many other signs in the presence of His disciples, which are not written in this book; but these are written that you may believe that Jesus is the Christ, the Son of God, and that believing you may have life in His name.

There is nothing in the Bible that declares Jesus came to show us the way to our higher consciousness or treasure-map our lives unto health, wealth, and happiness. He came to give his life as a ransom, and you can rejoice in this.

I cannot stress enough the importance of understanding the difference between believing *in* God and *believing* God. With the exception of atheists, everyone believes *in* God. The question is do you *believe* God? When you are told by Jesus himself that unless you repent, you will perish (Luke 13:3, 5), do you believe it? There's a big difference between believing the firefighter who knocks on your door who declares the fire is near and not believing him. If you believe him, you will act accordingly. To me, there is no greater verse that clearly spells out the difference between believing God and merely believing in him than John 3:36, "He who believes in the Son has everlasting life; and he who does not believe the Son shall not see life, but the wrath of God abides on him."

My Life Since Being Rescued from the New Age

What a contrast!

For the first thirty-one years of my life,

o   I believed I was controlling my life through my thoughts,
o   I'd reincarnate over and over again,
o   I believed in the mighty power within just waiting to bring me whatever I wanted, and
o   I believed was an "old soul."

For the last twenty-nine years of my life,

o   I've lived with the knowledge that all my sins have been forgiven and removed from my account by faith in the work of Christ on my behalf (Rom. 8:1, 1 John 1:7);
o   I now possess eternal life and righteousness of Jesus Christ imputed to me by his grace (Rom. 5:1, 2 Cor. 5:21);
o   my life and every single event in it is ordained by the Living God (Ps. 139); and
o   because of his grace, he is *for* me, and he alone knows and does what is best for me:
    ▪   "The Lord will perfect that which concerns me" (Ps. 138:8).
    ▪   "I will cry out to God Most High, to God who performs all things for me" (Ps. 57:2).

- "But as for me, I trust in You, O Lord; I say, "You are my God." 15 My times are in Your hand" (Ps. 31:14–15).
- "Do not fear, little flock, for it is your Father's good pleasure to give you the kingdom" (Luke 12:32).

From the moment of my conversion right up to this present time, my life is filled with joy. Just as with everybody else, there are good days and challenging days. Becoming a believer doesn't make us a Pollyanna. I'm not 100 percent positive all the time. I still complain and grumble, lose my temper, etc. But that's because I'm still a fallen sinner. But praise be to God, I am a redeemed sinner! When I find myself grumbling, I'm blessed to (as one of my favorite pastors puts it) "preach the gospel to myself every day." How? For me, I turn to my favorite chapter in the Bible, the one I read that opened my eyes all those years ago—the fifth chapter of Romans.

> For when we were still without strength, in due time *Christ died for the ungodly.* For scarcely for a righteous man will one die; yet perhaps for a good man someone would even dare to die. *But God demonstrates His own love toward us, in that while we were still sinners, Christ died for us.* Much more then, having now been justified by His blood, *we shall be saved from wrath through Him.* For if when we were enemies we were reconciled to God through the death of His Son, much more, having been reconciled, we shall be saved by His life. And not only that, but we also rejoice in God through our Lord Jesus Christ, through whom we have now received the reconciliation. (Rom 5:6–11; italics added)

These words melt me every time as do these gems from Ephesians 2:4–5, 7–10.

> God, who is rich in mercy, *because of His great love with which He loved us, even when we were dead* [italics added] in trespasses, *made us alive* [italics added] together with Christ (by grace you have been saved).

> That in the ages to come *He might show the exceeding riches of His grace in His kindness toward us in Christ Jesus* [italics added]. For *by grace you have been saved through faith* [italics added], and that not of yourselves; *it is the gift of God* [italics added], not of works, lest anyone should boast. For we are His workmanship, created in Christ Jesus for good works, which God prepared beforehand that we should walk in them."

The lies I believed and practiced have been exposed. The New Age, though, teaches that *you* are in the driver's seat the whole time. In fact, it goes one step further. The New Ages says right now, you are constantly *speaking your reality into being*. You are actually manifesting whatever you are inwardly dwelling upon. Now if we're honest, this brings problems. It's safe to say unless you are all-knowing (and trust me, you're not!), the *last* thing you want is to always get your way. I'm a living proof.

Conversely, the optimism and joy that comes from the scriptures brings real peace because it's all true! And, dear friend, it is available to *anyone* and *everyone* who calls on the name of the Lord and asks him to save him from his sins.

The only life you have comes from God. It is not yours to trifle with.

We are creatures who are not only limited in our understanding but also *have fallen* in sin. According to the Bible, there are many who foolishly live by their hearts, feelings, and appearances. But our hearts and understanding are darkened. Scripture declares in Proverbs 14:12, "There is a way that seems right to a man but its end is the way of death." Even if we live by sound business judgment, we are still limited and liable to mistakes and poor choices. God, of course, is sinless, perfect, and has all the knowledge. Believe me, the *best* prayer you can pray (second only to the prayer for your salvation) is "Nevertheless, not my will but *your* will be done." God always knows and does what is right, and we do not own ourselves but rather are created and owned by the Almighty God. When Paul preached on Mars Hill, he said:

> God gives to all life, breath, and all things. And He has made from one blood every nation of men to dwell on all the face of the earth, and has determined their pre-appointed times and the boundaries of their dwellings, so that they should seek the Lord, in the hope that they might grope for Him and find Him, though He is not far from each one of us. (Acts 17:25–27)

We *want* God's will for our lives. His first will is our salvation, which he personally provides and applies to all who ask him in repentance and faith. Without it, we are doomed eternally. But with it, we are eternally secure. You live your life knowing that according to Scripture, nothing—*absolutely nothing*—can separate us from the love of God in Christ Jesus, our Lord (Rom. 8:39). But we must come to God on his terms, not ours. Secondly it is God's will that we grow and mature in our faith. 1 Thessalonians 4:3 declares, "For this is the will of God, your sanctification." Second Peter 3:18 says, "Grow in the grace and knowledge of our Lord and Savior Jesus Christ." And 1 Peter 2:2 says, "As newborn babes, desire the pure milk of the word that you may grow thereby…"

I've come to realize there are four views we can take of ourselves:

1. *There's the person we think we are.* We all have an opinion and view of ourselves that we believe to be true. This is always subject to change and may nor may not be true, but we certainly believe it to be so.
2. There's the person *others* think we are. People form opinions of us that may or may not align with who we think we are.
3. There's the person *we think* others think we are. We believe we are seen by others in a certain light that may or may not be true.
4. *There's the person God says we are.* Of all viewpoints, this one is the only one that matters because *it's the only one that is true.* God says we are sinners in need of redemption due to both original sin and actual sin. When he saved us, he saw us as adopted into his family and saved. If we are not saved, then our sin condemns us forever. What makes the difference? Our pride. If we feel we don't need saving, we are deceived. If we humble ourselves and ask him to save us, we are saved.

There are no do-overs on this. There is no reincarnation.

"But, what if you're wrong, Taylor?" you ask. That is an absolutely fair question, so I'll repeat it again. *I'm not your mother.* You are free to believe whatever you like. I'll only say that if I'm wrong, then *God has lied* and I've placed 100 percent of my dependence upon a lie. Happily, Scripture tells us God *does not* lie (Num. 23:19, 1 Sam. 15:29, Titus 1:2, Heb. 6:18).

The Holy Scriptures are more than able to withstand scrutiny. You would be hard-pressed to find anything in the scriptures that even remotely suggests they are to be metaphysically interpreted.

On one hand, you have the myriad of New Age beliefs and books and conferences on the following:

• The laws of cause and effect to create your richly deserved life of health, wealth, and happiness

- The teaching of the mighty power within from our higher selves and God-spark
- Reincarnations, including karmic consequences
- Past-life regression therapies
- Star children
- Astral projection
- Ascended masters of the Far East

On the other hand, you have the Holy Scriptures proclaiming our single greatest hope of rescue from our fallen sinful state, without which we would be forever doomed—redemption.

> I determined not to know anything among you except Jesus Christ and Him crucified. (1 Cor. 2:2)

As the hymn says, "My hope is built on nothing less than Jesus's blood and righteousness."

What a contrast—the tantalizing baubles and imaginary victories of reaching the higher consciousness with all that it offers and the stark warning from the words of Jesus himself from Mark 8:36, "What will it profit a man if he gains the whole world, and loses his own soul?"

I'm not betting my soul and dependence on *anyone's interpretation* of Scripture. I'd rather trust that the Bible says what it means and means what it says because it is inspired by God. When the Bible uses parables, it says so and also explains those parables. I don't need a codebook to explain it. When the Bible uses hyperbole, I accept it as hyperbole. Ever heard someone say, "I'm so hungry I could eat a horse"? That's hyperbole. When Jesus tells us that if our eye causes us to sin, we should pluck it out and cast it from us or if our hand causes us to sin, we should cut it off and cast it away, he's using hyperbole to describe the proper abhorrence of sinning against a holy God.

When the Bible uses narrative and historical events I accept them as such. When Jesus walked on water, I believe he actually did so because that's what the Bible says! I don't need a *Metaphysical*

Bible Dictionary to tell me that the water represents our emotions and that when our divine spark is prominent, it too conquers our emotions and brings peace. That's all stuff that's been added by people who are not authorized to add or subtract anything from Scripture. There is no authority whatsoever to spiritualize and allegorize events to fit our particular views. Unity and all false religions are masters at this.

But Unity and all of the New Age are mere puppets. Ask yourself who's *really* the author behind all the adding, subtracting, spiritualizing, allegorizing, and misinterpreting. None other than the devil himself, whom Scripture calls the adversary and the Great Deceiver.

The Bible distinguishes between *three kinds of life* and *three kinds of death*. There is *physical life, spiritual life, and eternal life.* Likewise, there is *physical death, spiritual death, and eternal death.*

Despite what the New Age would have us to believe, according to the Bible, we come into this world *physically alive but spiritually dead.* If we remain in this condition upon physical death, we immediately *experience eternal death.* This is the damnation of the soul in torment, flames, darkness, separation from God, weeping, and gnashing of teeth. There is no recovery from this.

However, when during our physical lifetime, we come to Christ, confessing our sins of disobedience, trusting in his work on our behalf, and asking his forgiveness, we instantly are given *spiritual life*; and upon our physical death, we are ushered into *eternal life* and everlasting joy.

Since being rescued from the lies of the New Age and saved by the grace and blood of Christ, I have had the privilege over the past twenty-nine years to serve in various ministries, whether leading weekly home fellowship groups, serving as a worship leader, to becoming an ordained preaching elder with the desire to accurately present and proclaim the Gospel.

For the past several years to the present, I've been blessed to head the retirement community ministry in my local church where we bring the Gospel of free grace into retirement homes for those unable to attend church. This is by far the most rewarding ministry I've ever been pleased to serve in. I recall the latter days of my mother's life when she too lived in such a community. I'd go to visit her and would be grieved to see literature from the damnable cults. It is a great honor and privilege to direct these dear old souls to the throne of grace.

For many in these communities, it is the last time they'll hear the Gospel. To my great joy, many of the residents are believers. What a delight to exhort and encourage them in the faith, and I look forward to continuing in this ministry for as long as the Lord wills. For nearly all of the year 2020, a pandemic has closed down retirement communities from outside visitors. Mercifully I am still able to preach through my private YouTube channel, which broadcasts directly into the rooms of residents.

To the believers reading this book, continue in the faith, and continue praying for your friends who are not yet saved. You'll never know on this side of heaven how many people your example will touch. I remember hearing a pastor once say, "Your life may be the first Bible anyone may ever read." He meant that we are to walk the walk. When a person offends someone and asks for their forgiveness, it speaks volumes to a fallen world. There's a difference between "I'm sorry" and "Will you please forgive me?"

To those reading this who are not saved or are part of a group that has departed from what the scriptures teach, please consider that. To quote Jonathan Edwards, "Friend, the only reason that you have not plunged headlong into hell from the moment you stepped out of your bed this morning is owing to the mere mercy of God who holds you up." Please heed these words, and ask Christ to save you. There is no magic formula. James 4:10 says, "Humble yourselves in the sight of the Lord, and He will lift you up." And Jesus declares, "And the tax collector, standing afar off, would not so much as raise his eyes to heaven, but beat his breast, saying, 'God, be merciful to me a sinner!' I tell you, this man went down to his house justified" (Luke 18:13–14).

I will close this book with the *four absolute truths* I close every sermon with. These are real truths and not my interpretation of anything since all four points come straight from the pages of the Holy

Scriptures and are borrowed from the late Dr. James Montgomery Boice:

1. Your sins will damn you, and you are unable to extricate yourself from them.
   - "The wages of sin is death" (Rom. 6:23).
     - o Wages are earned by completing the task. We've all earned death due to our habitual task of sinning. Because we are dead spiritually, we must be delivered. We need a Savior to do this for us. *Savior* literally means "deliverer." That Deliverer is Jesus himself. Colossians 1:13–14 states, "He has delivered us from the power of darkness and conveyed us into the kingdom of the Son of His love, in whom we have redemption through His blood, the forgiveness of sins."
   - We are *already* cursed, and here's proof:
     - o "Cursed is everyone who does not continue in all things which are written in the book of the law, to do them" (Gal. 3:10).
     - o This leaves no doubt. This verse says that without exception, everybody who is not *performing everything* the Bible's commands right now and forevermore is cursed. Absolute, perpetual obedience is commanded, not merely "meaning well" or trying or not performing some things only. If you are not performing absolute perpetual obedience right now, you are cursed.
2. Jesus is a perfect Savior who rescues us by *performing in our stead and bearing our punishment.*
   - "Christ *has redeemed us* from the curse of the law, having become a curse for us" (Gal. 3:13; italics added).
   - "For God made Jesus who knew no sin to be sin for us, that we might become the righteousness of God in Him" (2 Cor. 5:21).

- "For Christ also suffered once for sins, the just for the unjust, that He might bring us to God" (1 Pet. 3:18).
3. Jesus accepts anyone and everyone who comes to him on his terms.
    - "For God so loved the world that He gave His only begotten Son, that whoever believes in Him should not perish but have everlasting life" (John 3:16).
    - "Come to Me, all you who labor and are heavy laden, and I will give you rest" (Matt. 11:28).
    - "Now then, we are ambassadors for Christ, as though God were pleading through us: we implore you on Christ's behalf, be reconciled to God" (2 Cor. 5:20).
4. The only terms Christ accepts are *repentance* and *faith*.
    - "The time is fulfilled, and the kingdom of God is at hand. Repent, and believe in the gospel" (Mark 1:15; italics added).
    - "He who covers his sins will not prosper, but whoever confesses and forsakes them will have mercy" (Prov. 28:13; italics added).
    - "I will deliver you from the Jewish people, as well as from the Gentiles, to whom I now send you, to open their eyes, in order to turn them from darkness to light, and from the power of Satan to God, that they may receive forgiveness of sins and an inheritance among those who are sanctified by faith in Me" (Acts 26:17–18; italics added).
    - "Testifying both to the Jews, and also to the Greeks, repentance toward God, and faith toward our Lord Jesus Chris" (Acts 20:21 NKJV; italics added).
    - "Repent therefore and be converted, that your sins may be blotted out, so that times of refreshing may come from the presence of the Lord" (Acts 3:18–19; italics added).
    - "Most assuredly, I say to you, he who hears My word and believes in Him who sent Me has everlasting life,

and shall not come into judgment, but has passed from death into life" (John 5:24).

- "The word is near you, in your mouth and in your heart" (that is, the word of faith which we preach): that if you confess with your mouth the Lord Jesus and believe in your heart that God has raised Him from the dead, you will be saved. For with the heart one believes unto righteousness, and with the mouth confession is made unto salvation. For the Scripture says, 'Whoever believes on Him will not be put to shame.' For there is no distinction between Jew and Greek, for the same Lord over all is rich to all who call upon Him. For 'whoever calls on the name of the Lord shall be saved'" (Rom. 10:8–13).

May the Lord be pleased in using this book for the blessing, encouraging, strengthening, salvation, and warning of many.

Taylor and His Father 1965

Taylor Bassett family

About the Author

Taylor Bassett was raised as a Truth student and ardently practiced the belief system known as the New Age for the first half of his life until his conversion to Christianity at the age of thirty-one. Since then, Taylor has led numerous Bible studies, was ordained as an elder, and continues sharing the Gospel of free grace every Sunday as an itinerant preacher. Taylor and his wife, Laura, have been married since 1993 and they have six children together. They are members of Grace Bible Church in Escondido, California.

CPSIA information can be obtained
at www.ICGtesting.com
Printed in the USA
BVHW071236110621
609348BV00004B/598